# THE GRAVE WALL

**Wendy Wilburn and Dave Dye**

D1416034

ISBN: 1470013649
ISBN-13: 9781470013646
LCCN: 2012902120
CreateSpace, North Charleston, SC

# THE PROLOGUE

I was in a bad place, spiritually and emotionally, in December 2008, as my 47th birthday approached. What had happened to my life? It was difficult to remember the last time I truly felt happy and at peace. I desperately wanted that feeling back.

I hadn't seen or heard from my husband, Taruk Ben-Ali, in 4 1/2 years. His father, Hassan, insisted that Taruk had left me and moved on with his life, either out of state or even out of the country. Hassan's story changed several times. It was still a mystery to me because no one else had seen or spoken to Taruk since I talked to him on June 8, 2004. He had just vanished.

Hassan acted as if he knew his son's whereabouts. I just kept trying to come to grips with the reality that I would be spending the rest of my life without the man I considered my soul mate, and I didn't know exactly why.

Meanwhile, my father had been diagnosed with the beginning stages of Alzheimer's and had temporarily moved into my home in Hayward, CA. It was going to be a difficult struggle for him and a challenge for all of us. I had gotten a call one night from the police back in Southfield, MI., telling me that he was no longer capable of living by himself. I flew back to pick him up so he could come live with me, but I was dreading what it would be like to watch him deteriorate with this awful disease. He was so different from the strong man who had raised me, the rock that I thought was so invincible.

My career also had been in disarray the last few months. I had worked for eight years in sales and marketing for a company that owned hotels and other businesses worldwide. But things changed quickly when the company realigned and my boss got reassigned. I started reporting to someone else and, even though I consistently met my sales goals, it was clear that this man wanted to run me out. He made my life a living hell for no apparent reason and, eventually, I did leave the company in October.

So, I was out of work, in therapy, a nervous wreck and not certain where things were headed for me and my 16-year-old son, Jordan. It was a terrible time of uncertainty, a week before Christmas.

Thank God for Jordan. He kept my spirits up as much as anyone or anything could under the circumstances.

The morning of December 18th started off so perfectly. Jordan was already in the shower getting ready for school when I woke up. That might sound like a little thing, but to me, it was a very big little thing that particular morning. I often had to battle to get him up and going. This time, much to my surprise, he was already a step ahead of me.

It gave me a little extra time to make a much-needed coffee run. I threw on a jacket, slipped on my sandals and drove to the nearest 7-11.

Much to my delight, they had my favorite, rarely-found flavor in stock - Banana Foster. Yum.

This was like java paradise for me. The little things, you know.

It's odd, because I've asked for that flavor every time since, and they've never had it again. This was the one and only time that I've seen it there.

Moments like that make me believe, more and more, in the little things in life. When you're hurting deep down, when so much is seemingly falling apart around you, the little things can give you hope. They can put a smile on your face, distract you from the heartache of life's realities, even if only briefly, and give you a shot of energy to keep going.

Maybe that Banana Foster was supposed to be a nice little treat that was meant just for me that morning, because the day was soon going to turn horrific.

After what we'd been through over the last few years, any small favor - even my son getting out of bed on his own and a delicious cup of coffee - felt like a blessing.

I was on the way home, sipping and savoring my Banana Foster, when the cell phone started buzzing. The caller ID read: "Sue Johnson."

What did she want this time? I really didn't want to ruin a good start to the day by picking up, but I knew that I had to answer, just in case.

"Are you watching the news?" Sue said frantically. "Turn on Channel 2. Brace yourself."

"I'm in the car," I told her. "What is it?"

"Just hurry up, get home and turn on the TV," she said before hanging up.

My splendid morning suddenly became nerve-racking. All I could think was, "What is happening now? What next?"

It couldn't be good, that much was for sure. Not coming from Sue. She wouldn't call me with good news. That's not Sue.

The last couple miles home seemed like they took forever. So many thoughts were racing through my mind.

I ran inside, slipping and nearly falling in the entryway, as I headed straight to my bedroom to turn on the television.

I looked up and immediately dropped the cup of coffee. I could not believe what I saw.

"Police are investigating the strange discovery of an entombed body in an apartment building," the reporter said. "The body was found in the 2200 block of Ashby Avenue. Whose body and how it got there are some of the questions this morning."

I knew exactly whose body it was.

It was my husband's.

And I knew how it got there, too. His father put him there.

I've actually gotten to where I rarely watch the news anymore. It's always so depressing. Just one horror story after another.

Only this time was a lot different. This time, the horror story involved me.

Three days earlier, Taruk's father had committed suicide. Since then, there had been rumors about a dead body possibly being hidden in this apartment building, which Taruk owned, and where his dad, mom and step-dad all lived.

A woman named Hasira, a female friend of Hassan's, had come forward in recent days with information for the police.

But I hadn't given any credibility to Hasira's story. She was a little kooky in my opinion. Never in the world did I think the police would even follow up on her tip. It seemed so absurd.

But as I was watching this bizarre scene unfold, I said to myself, "Oh my God, she was telling the truth."

I was in total disbelief, couldn't breathe. The video made me sick to my stomach.

Taruk's father and I had never gotten along. He hated me. I thought he was neurotic, downright evil at times, but I never imagined that he was this sick and twisted.

Since Taruk had vanished more than four years earlier, I never wanted to be around that apartment building anymore. Taruk and I used to call it "Ashby Arms." It was our cute little pet name, but there was nothing cute about it anymore.

My thoughts kept bouncing around. I had memory after memory of Taruk while also trying to make sense of how and why this happened.

All the while, I was trying to listen to the TV. A police officer told the reporter, "As far as determining an age at this point, due to the decomposition of the body, it's going to take us a little bit more time."

Sue Johnson, divorced from Hassan for many years, had been calling me frequently over the previous few days, which was why I was hesitant to answer her call. We weren't best friends by any means. I didn't really trust her, just didn't think she was forthright. I'd heard too many stories from Taruk about how unstable his family life had been growing up.

Sue apparently had decided recently that she wanted to be in good with me. It was all very fake, almost laughable. She evidently thought I would be inheriting the apartment building at some point and she wanted her piece of the pie. I guess she had believed what Hasira told the police and had put the puzzle together faster than I did. Or maybe Sue knew the truth all along, or at least suspected it. Who knows?

The next thing I remember seeing on the television was the fire department's hazardous material team, wearing full biohazard suits, bringing several red plastic bags full of evidence out of the building.

Then came the image I'll never get out of my mind for as long as I live. A six-foot-long box that looked like a home-made coffin was carried out.

Inside that box was my husband, God rest his soul.

After years of wondering why he'd left, where he had gone, the truth was finally playing out repulsively right before my eyes.

I guess I could have gone the rest of my life not knowing what had really happened to Taruk. That limbo had been so incredibly difficult for me to handle. I didn't think anything could be worse.

But there obviously was something worse, much worse. I felt that I needed closure, but I didn't need this type of closure.

Poor Taruk. He was 36 years old when he went missing. He had his issues, including an off-and-on drug problem, but he didn't deserve this.

They just kept replaying the video of the crime scene on the newscast. The TV anchor said, "Sources who have been inside the building confirm the body was discovered behind an elaborately built false wall and say the body may have been packed in dirt."

Just then my son entered the room. His eyes were red and tears were pouring down his cheeks.

I thought he had already left for school, but he had been watching, too. He heard me and turned on his television.

I started sobbing uncontrollably. Jordan hugged me tighter than he had ever hugged me before.

"My dad is really dead." He said it over and over. "My dad is really dead."

Taruk wasn't Jordan's biological father, but he had become a father figure to him, and a good one.

I honestly never prepared myself for this outcome. I had been adamant that I wouldn't go through with a divorce, even when his dad tried to talk me into it, because I was going to force Taruk to face me.

I had even joked with friends, "He'll have to prove he was abducted by aliens for me to forgive him."

I never even contacted police to report Taruk as a missing person because I never considered him missing.

I had no doubt that Hassan was lying about some of the details, but he told me that he'd been in contact with Taruk. "He's fine," Hassan would say. "He went to Vegas," or "He's moving to Mexico."

The location kept changing, but I assumed that was just Hassan being Hassan, the pathological liar coming out.

Death never crossed my mind, not even when Hassan claimed the mob was chasing Taruk, one of the many explanations.

If Hassan suspected foul play, wouldn't he have said that so we could get the police involved?

For me to think that Taruk was dead, I would have had to think his dad killed him and hid his body in a wall or something. Who could have imagined such a thing would happen in real life, my life?

It was all so hard to grasp, especially the shock of watching it unfold on TV. I tried to comfort Jordan, but I don't think I was much help. He helped me more than I helped him. My mind was spinning out of control.

My father adored Taruk, thought he was a stand-up guy, but with his dementia, I don't think he completely understood what I was telling him. He was sympathetic, but there was so little emotion. It was as if I was telling him that a neighbor down the street had died, not my husband.

When I called my mom, she couldn't even understand what I was saying at first because I was so distraught.

After she finally pieced together the details, I remember her telling me, "This doesn't happen in normal society. This stuff only happens in backwood hills."

At some point, I can't even remember when, Jordan decided that he would go to school for the last part of the day. I don't know how he did it. I was such a mess, I just let him go.

The one person I thought could help me at a time like this was my best friend, Gina Taylor, who knew Taruk well and even lived with us for a brief time.

I went over to her place and we shared some memories. We cried. We laughed. We cried some more.

And then we went and got drunk.

I kept thinking back to the last time I'd seen Taruk, my best friend, my partner, my husband. Never would I have thought that was going to be the last time I would ever see him.

It was a chilling realization on a day when the truth hurt more than ever.

# CHAPTER 1

Most parents can't wait for the day when their baby stops constantly crying so they can get a little sleep. My mother, Jan, was just the opposite. She wanted her daughter - me, Wendelyn Eyvonne Wilburn, born on December 12, 1960 - to cry in the worst possible way.

She feared that I was deaf. When I wasn't crying as a newborn, my mom thought it had to be because I wasn't hearing sounds. The nurses tried to assure her that I did indeed cry, but whenever I was around my mom, nothing. Complete silence.

That all changed as soon as we pulled into the driveway of our home at 1007 Fountain Street in Ann Arbor, MI. Then they say that I cried and cried and never stopped crying. My mother learned to be careful of what she wished for.

I enjoyed toys, just like any other kid, but not nearly as much as books. I loved to read. My favorite was the Winnie-the-Pooh series, so much so that my dad nicknamed me "Pooh." My older brother,

David, picked up on it, but with a slight variation. He called me "Wendy the Poop." Why are boys so mean to their younger sisters?

My father, Frank, was known for lecturing his three children, especially David and, of course, me. I learned to love that aspect of my dad. I experienced it to an extreme while preparing for my first day of school. Several times, my parents walked and drove the route to and from the school with me. My dad's final instruction, which he had repeatedly said, was simple: "Do NOT get in the car with strangers."

They  dropped me off at school on a practice run. I was to walk straight home. They told me that they'd see me in about seven minutes, drove off and I started walking. I must have been crying. Within seconds, a car drove by, slowed down, and asked if I was OK and needed a ride home. I said, "Sure," got in and let them drive me back to our house.

My parents were just getting out of their car when I popped out of this stranger's vehicle. My dad was furious and immediately started yelling at me. My mom said that there were "big crocodile tears" rolling down my face. I learned my lesson and never made that mistake again.

A couple years earlier, David was entering kindergarten. The parents were invited to attend a play/work station that the teacher had set up as an intro to the class, and I tagged along. When the walkthrough was completed, the parents were supposed to leave. I didn't want to leave. I started screaming and refused to go.

The principal heard me down the hall. For years, she told the story at this annual kindergarten intro about the 4-year-old who didn't want to leave school. My mom said that she thought my reaction was a sign of an independent thinker. The principal's message: Don't bring your younger children to the orientation.

In junior high, I was introduced to racism from both sides after kids were bused to my neighborhood school. I've got African American and Irish blood in me from my mom's side, German from my dad's and American Indian from both.

Friends have seen the photo of my mom on the wall in my house, and they think she looks like Halle Berry. Or, rather, Halle Berry looked like my mom, back in the day. I had never noticed the resemblance until they said that, but they're right. She did look like Halle Berry. In her younger days, my mom was a model at the car shows in Detroit. My dad was 6' 4", fair skinned and very intelligent, but a private man. She was a school teacher; he was an electrical engineer.

At school, the blacks didn't like me because I spoke differently from them, lived in a nice house and was light skinned with green eyes and sandy-colored hair. I was too white for them and they were mean to me.

I didn't fit in with the white kids, either. My mom always said, "One drop of black blood, and you're black."

I felt like I was stuck between a rock and a hard place. I eventually grew to have a deep interest in African American culture and history, and the struggle of black people in America.

Fortunately, there was another girl of color in my neighborhood and we became best friends. Debbie is a doctor now and still lives in Michigan. We don't talk or see each other, but I still love her. That friendship meant a lot to me, growing up.

I also had a few good friends from the neighborhood who were white. We eventually reconnected through Facebook.

But I struggled with why people were so hateful just because you looked or sounded a little different. I had no problem letting the narrow-minded ones know exactly what I thought of them and their views.

I turned to my grandmother, Mimi, my dad's mom, for some answers. She was white and I felt she understood me better than anybody. So I asked her why we were different. She didn't want to talk about it. It was the one and only time in my life when she got angry with me. Mimi said firmly, "Drop it." I did, but it didn't end my curiosity.

Some people might think that I had the "middle-child syndrome" growing up. David was athletic, tall, handsome, intelligent, and funny. He got all the attention. My younger brother, Trey, was always the baby. I was sort of stuck in the middle, lost in the shuffle, which maybe gave me more freedom.

My first real job was at Phillips Shoes at Briarwood Mall in Ann Arbor. It was the beginning of my love affair with shoes and shoe sales. You can't have enough shoes.

I swam competitively through ninth grade. My other hobbies included dance, choir, band (played the flute) and horseback riding.

For high school, I attended Ann Arbor Huron. We were the River Rats. Is that a classic mascot or what?

I was a cheerleader, played powder-puff football with the girls and was a self-proclaimed "social butterfly." One of my proudest moments came when my classmates selected me for the Homecoming Court.

I didn't have a boyfriend throughout high school. I think I was still too heartbroken from the break-up of my first love back in junior high. His name was Danny. He was the greatest person I had ever met - an athlete who was smart, fun and caring. We were best friends and we would talk on the phone for hours.

But my father made me break up with him because he thought that I was too young to be crazy about a boy like that. For no good reason, my dad didn't trust me. Having to break up with Danny broke my heart.

I compared everyone to him, and all relationships to ours. I soon became disillusioned about relationships, because I couldn't find that same combination, someone who made me feel the way Danny did.

My friends considered me the drug-and-alcohol police in high school. It was mostly just marijuana in those days. I lectured them on the dangers of drinking and smoking pot, and always made sure they got home safely when they were drunk or high.

My first beer didn't come until age 18. I have to admit, I liked it. I also tried pot, but didn't like that at all; it made me very nervous. My eyes looked crazed and I always asked friends, "Do I look high?" So I didn't experiment with it for long, just wasn't my thing.

I headed off to college and studied communications at Western Michigan in Kalamazoo, before transferring back to the University of Michigan in my hometown.

You might have heard of Kalamazoo. It's where they had some of those so-called Elvis sightings a couple of decades ago, which led to speculation that Elvis Presley had faked his death. If I was going to fake my death, I'd definitely end up someplace much warmer and without all that lake-effect snow. But that's just me.

My dream was to become a movie star or TV newscaster. I didn't become a star, obviously, but I did appear in two movies. The first was *Made in America,* a comedy released in 1993 that starred Whoopi Goldberg and Ted Danson and featured Will Smith and Nia Long. I heard they were looking for extras, so I showed up and got picked to be in the graduation scene.

The other film was *Carriers,* a horror flick that came out in 1988. It was a small-time film made and produced in Michigan, and premiered at the old Fifth Forum theatre in Ann Arbor. My mom saw it, and told me that it was an "OK" movie. I never did see it. There were no big-name stars. I played one of the monsters. One of my friends told me that I fit the role perfectly.

I did some runway modeling and hair shows over the years, too. My other claim to fame was singing bank-up on an Herb Albert album.

While Michigan always will be home, I made up my mind in December 1985 to go west and not look back. I remember staring out the window, watching the winter's first snowstorm whip furiously outside. That was the moment when I decided that I'd had enough. It would be my final winter in Michigan. Ready or not, the sun and fun of California were calling me.

Leaving your roots, saying goodbye to family and lifelong friends, is so difficult. That's your comfort zone.

In my case, it was all I had really known. Most of my friends thought that I was crazy to move so far, but I was 24, feisty and ready to break away. I had a good job lined up, a management position in the hotel industry. It was a solid career move with higher pay and more responsibility. My office was near the Pacific Ocean, in San Francisco Bay, overlooking the skyline. How can you top that?

While the winters had worn on me, I also felt that I'd outgrown Ann Arbor to some extent. I needed a change. My older brother had finished school and was living in Minnesota. My younger brother was up in East Lansing, going to school at Michigan State.

My mom had grown up in Indiana. My dad was from Detroit and only left Michigan when he was in the Air Force.

They had raised me to be independent, and I guess that side was coming out again. It was time for me to make a new start.

I touched down in San Francisco on August 24, 1986. I remember exactly what I was wearing. It had been a hot, humid day, with temperatures in the 90s, when I left Detroit Metro Airport. I had on a cute yellow-and-white floral summer dress with white pumps. I'd bought the shoes a month earlier during a trip to Mexico with my mom.

We had gone to visit my grandpa, who lived in Guadalajara for 25 years. He was 90 years old. To keep his U.S. citizenship, he would come back and stay with us in Michigan for a while each year. I felt it was important to see him again before I moved. I didn't know how many more chances I'd get once I started my new job.

As excited as I was to make this move to California, there were some immediate second thoughts upon arrival. I definitely wasn't dressed for the weather. It was 50 degrees when we landed at around 10 p.m., which felt like below zero to me, coming out of the summer heat in the Midwest.

It was a quick reality check, an initiation into this not-so-warm-and-sunny Northern California. I guess I was expecting Los Angeles or San Diego weather.

I felt an initial letdown, but ended up living on the east side of the bay, near Oakland, which was a little warmer. It didn't take long for the Bay Area to win my heart. The picturesque beauty of the ocean was stunning. It was unlike anything I'd ever seen before.

If I ever questioned my decision to move again, all I had to do was step outside and take in that breathtaking, postcard scenery. My doubts quickly vanished.

My career took off. I even built up my own business, got married and settled down. My son, Jordan, was born in 1993. He looks just like me, except with dimples and thick eyebrows - an up-graded version.

His father, Ric, was charming in the beginning and I fell for it. He was 6' 2" and a few pounds over-weight. Still, I thought he was fairly attractive. The red undertones in his medium coloring showed the Indian in his background.

But the marriage was a mistake. He was a fake, a square, and a workaholic. He lied to me constantly and really didn't want to be a father at all. It was such a huge disappointment. While stable and reliable in some ways, Ric was a horrible husband and father.

I would ask for parental help in certain situa-tions, and he never came through. We separated for good when Jordan was 3 1/2. At the time, Ric said that he preferred to wait until Jordan was a teenager to get involved as a father. Excuse me? I never did quite figure that one out. He stuck to his word, though, and became a classic deadbeat dad.

Being a single parent obviously isn't easy, es-pecially with my entire family a couple thousand miles away.

I got involved in an abusive relationship and was seriously questioning my choices. But I didn't give up all hope of meeting the right man someday. There's another "Danny" out there somewhere, I told myself.

Not just for me but for Jordan, too. He needed a father figure in his life.

I had no clue when I'd find that perfect person for me, and for us, but I believed it would happen.

At the same time, I couldn't afford another mistake like I'd made with my first marriage. I tried not to worry about a timetable, even though Jordan was getting to an age where he was going to need a positive male influence.

# CHAPTER 2

It's such an intriguing phenomenon the way someone comes into your life at a certain time. Take a left turn and you meet your soul mate. Take a right turn and maybe you miss him.

Timing is everything. How often have you felt a connection with somebody but it was just a bad time for you or a bad time for them?

One person just had their heart broken and it's too soon to start over. Another person is still in a dying relationship and hasn't figured out their exit strategy. So, you both move on, wondering what might have been if you had met at a different time —maybe a year earlier, maybe a year later.

A soul mate is defined as "a person with whom one has a feeling of deep and natural affinity, similarity, love, intimacy, sexuality, spirituality or compatibility."

You have no idea when you're going to meet the person who fits that description for you. Look up at just the right moment to make eye contact with someone and it could be the beginning of the greatest thing that's ever happened in your life. Or, maybe, the start of the worst.

Sometimes, as I did, you open the package and get both.

It was 1998. I'd been settled into the Bay Area for 12 years. Gas was $1.15 a gallon, Google had just been founded and President Bill Clinton was saying, "I never had sexual relations with Monica Lewinsky."

I was 37, still a single mom, living with Jordan in Berkeley, CA on the border of Oakland. My top priority was to find a quality education for him, which wasn't easy to do in that area.

I'd grown up in a college town. I guess it's only logical that school systems are going to be better in that type of environment. The schools I went to - Thurston Elementary, Clague Middle School and Huron High - all received 9's or 10's in the GreatSchools.org rankings. The schools where I was living in California have ratings of five and below.

Sending Jordan, who was 5 years old, off to kindergarten under those circumstances was a little stressful. I had little or no faith in the school system that I was entrusting with my son's future. It was a terrible feeling, especially for someone who was raised in an academic family.

My mom had been a school teacher. I could remember her saying that the parents who were always around the school, poking their noses in and asking questions, would get on the teachers' nerves. They were sort of the watch dogs. The teachers knew someone was following their every move. It kept them on their toes.

I decided that I was going to be one of those types of parents. I would hang around and keep a close eye on my son, the teachers, and the administration.

I signed up to be a volunteer. I went on all the field trips and helped out in the activities room. More importantly, I could keep track of Jordan and monitor his social skills. I was in his classroom for a while nearly every day.

When the principal found out that my background included working with caterers, she asked me to organize a luncheon. The event went smoothly. A few days later, I was in the principal's office, where she personally thanked me. She said that I helped to make her look good, because the lunch was a success. It felt like we were becoming close friends. There was some mutual respect and trust developing.

Just as she was thanking me, we got interrupted. It was an interruption that would change my life for the better and, eventually, for the worse.

At her office door stood a tall, probably 6' 1", muscular, stunning man with warm eyes. I'll never forget those eyes. I can see them to this day, and that makes me smile.

I couldn't initially pinpoint his nationality, perhaps Latino, but he was so handsome.

I always tell my girlfriends, "We choose the man; the man does not choose us."

Well, I was choosing him right there, right then.

Here we were in an elementary school with my son down the hall, and I felt like a little school girl with an instant crush. We shared a smile. He had a quick word with the principal and off he went.

"Oh well," I thought to myself, "probably for the best."

I was in a really bad relationship at the time. I wanted out, but it wasn't that easy. The man just wasn't letting go, and I was becoming more and more terrified of him.

I decided this crazy crush wasn't meant to be. Easy come, easy go.

Or so I thought.

A few days later, I was standing on the stairs, waiting for Jordan after school, when once again, out of nowhere, appeared this man whom I'd seen in the principal's office. Who was he? What's his deal?

This time, I would find out. He walked up, extended his hand and said, "Hi, my name's Taruk."

We shared some small talk. He was articulate and lively. I found out that he was a counselor at the school. Then he asked me if I liked hiking.

I said, "Yes, of course."

The question could have been, "Do you like jumping off bridges?"

"Yes, of course."

We exchanged phone numbers and Taruk promised that we would talk soon.

I couldn't wait, but I had a couple of concerns. First of all, I had told a small fib. I knew nothing about hiking, and I didn't even know if I had the appropriate shoes or boots to wear. I was pretty sure those white pumps I was wearing when I landed in California weren't going to get the job done.

What's worse, I knew that I was flirting with danger. I wasn't the type to cheat on someone, but this was different. I didn't want to be in this other relationship at all. His name was Shane. I was still seeing him a little, more out of fear than anything.

I had no idea what he might do if he found out I had gone on a date with someone else. I thought he might be capable of some bad things. It scared me, which is why I hadn't been able to totally break away from him in the first place.

I gave it a lot of thought and finally decided, heck with it, I'm moving on. Not only was Taruk handsome, he was charming. And there seemed to be such a warmth to him. I could sense it. I could feel it in his handshake. I could see it in his eyes, hear it in his voice.

About a week later, Taruk called. He had such an appealing telephone voice. I could listen to him forever. He seemed genuine to me, too, strong and determined, full of energy.

We decided to go shopping for a school project that was coming up in the art lab. Perfect idea. It was work related, which made it seem totally innocent, but it was still a great opportunity to get to know each other a little better.

What a blast we had. We turned something so simple into a real adventure. I swear I felt that I had known this man my whole life. I guess that's what it's like when people say they've met their soul mate.

Taruk told me that he had seen me at the luncheon and knew that day that he had to get to know me. I was flattered. I think I blushed. I hadn't even seen him there, but in this case, it was great to be seen.

Our second so-called date involved him helping me move some heavy boxes out of a storage area. Not real exciting, but he was a prince about it.

He asked me if I wanted to observe what he described as his "detention" class. I thought detention was a little extreme for grade-school kids, so I became curious about what exactly he did.

We set up a time for me to visit. A few days later, I knocked on the door to his classroom. He opened it, invited me in and started to introduce me. "This is Ms. Wil....."

He didn't get to finish my name. I looked up and shrieked, "Jor-dan!"

Jordan yelled back, "Mom?" almost like a panicky question.

I was stunned.

"Is that your son?" Taruk asked.

Yes, that was my kindergarten son in a detention class, sitting in the circle, which I guess meant that he was super-duper bad. Here I was, a volunteer at the school, and I had absolutely no clue.

Jordan looked horrified. His face was priceless. A combination of shock, fear and bewilderment.

The three of us went into the hallway to talk privately. Taruk was embarrassed that he hadn't made the connection between Jordan and I before this awkward incident. He explained that Jordan was a nice kid but did a little too much talking in class.

I wonder who he got that from?

I was a little upset with Jordan, but it wasn't that big of a deal. I was more angry that no one at the school had informed me. I was there every day. That was the whole idea behind volunteering. Shouldn't someone have tipped me off that my son was in trouble for disrupting class?

I decided right there that I was going to take him out of that school. I would move as soon as I could find a new place. I just couldn't get over the fact that I was volunteering there, had what I thought was a great relationship with the principal, and no one filled me in on this small detail.

I just thought it was a bad sign. I didn't want him in that school anymore for that reason and others.

It had become clear why this place had such a poor rating. It took them a year to realize that one of their teachers hadn't even graduated from college. They didn't do the proper background checks before hiring. How is that possible?

Jordan's teacher was about 90 years old and totally out of touch. It's no surprise that the atmosphere in that class was not conducive to learning.

After Christmas break, Jordan didn't go back there. I enrolled him in another school for the start of second semester.

Unfortunately, it also meant that Taruk and I didn't run into each other anymore. We basically lost contact for probably 15 months or so. I still thought about him occasionally. But it clearly wasn't the right time for me.

I was still going through hell trying to get out of this other relationship with Shane anyway. The man eventually began stalking me. I had to contact police and even moved to make sure I protected myself and my son.

It really felt as if we were on the run, hoping to find some calmness and stability far away from Shane. By the summer of 2000, I was ready to move again. It was the only way I felt any semblance of security, even if it was seemingly short-term.

Shane and I had been together for about a year. He was 5'10", in great physical condition, and light skinned with a nice smile. But it started to become apparent after nine months or so that he was not emotionally stable. He became jealous for no reason and was very controlling. He trashed my apartment after I went out with my girlfriends and spent a night at one of their houses. That was just the beginning.

Another night, Shane started screaming my name from outside when I didn't answer, and then he busted out the windows in my car.

The next time, he shot himself in his leg in the parking lot. I never did find out exactly why he had come to my apartment complex with a gun that night. I could only imagine.

It was also not uncommon for him to show up at my work unannounced, which usually led to a heated argument between us. The police were called a few times and he was taken to jail. He ended up stalking me like this for two years.

Even though moving is such an ordeal, I felt like I had to keep doing it from time to time. It was the best way to try to avoid Shane, who seemed ready to completely snap at any moment.

The first person I thought of when I was ready to move again was Taruk. I remember exactly what day it was - Aug. 14, 2000 - because it was his birthday. He was 32 years old.

So after all those months of never seeing him or hearing from him, I decided to give him a call. He had told me that he owned an apartment complex in Berkeley. I was hoping maybe he had a vacancy.

Great excuse for getting back in contact with him, don't you think?

I dialed his number, but a female answered. Not the kind of voice I wanted to hear, that's for sure.

"Oh, I'm his mother," the woman said. "He doesn't live here anymore, but let me give you his new number."

I immediately dialed it and Taruk answered. It felt great to hear his voice again. I absolutely loved that voice.

I wished him a happy birthday and inquired about any open apartments.

"Oh my god, I can't believe I'm hearing from you," he said. "I've been thinking about you. I lost your number. I don't have any units available, but I am. When can I see you?"

Great line, huh? I've heard a few pick-up lines over the years that made me want to get sick, but this one sounded quite a bit more sincere, at least to me. And it was humorous. I liked that. You know, laughing again. For the longest time, Jordan had been the only one who made me smile or laugh, who made me happy.

That was the moment when it all started up again. Even after a year and a half with no communication, I could still feel a chemistry, a connection between us. This was no infatuation. There was something there. I could feel it. I sensed that he did, too.

It wasn't so simple, though. I soon found out that he was living with another woman at the time, a friend of his whose name was Rhoda.

In retrospect, it was just another red flag that I chose to ignore.

I also started to learn some details about Taruk's shady past. During the time I hadn't seen or heard from him, while I was trying to get away from Shane, Taruk had spent several months in jail for dumping hazardous waste.

His dad apparently had some stuff from the building - paint cans, whatever it was - and asked Taruk to get rid of it. Taruk dumped it near the Berkeley Marina, not far from the apartment complex he owned.

He didn't go about it very smartly, either. Taruk's name and address were printed right on one of the boxes. Duh.

He ended up spending about six months in jail, which was why he was living with Rhoda. He was put on probation when he got out and needed a place to stay. His mom had been in the hospital and in rehab following a serious illness. She nearly died. So Rhoda offered him a room at her place.

Taruk and I started seeing each other on occasion, just hanging out, hiking, talking, going to movies, and really getting to know each other better.

The situation with Rhoda was uncomfortable for me, though. She and I eventually became cordial years later, after Taruk helped her to get a job. But I knew that she loved him and wanted to be in a relationship. It just wasn't mutual. Taruk didn't have those types of feelings for her. But they were certainly good friends.

I understood the situation. But I wasn't crazy about the whole arrangement. What woman would be?

I finally told him, "Regardless of why you're there, I'm not comfortable with it. You live with another woman. I don't want to get any more emotionally involved when I don't know what's going to happen."

I had no idea how much this was going to bother him, but I told him that I didn't want to see him anymore.

He immediately acknowledged it did bother him, and it bothered him a lot.

I left things this way: "When you're no longer living with another woman, give me a call. Until then, I'm not interested."

That conversation took place around Thanksgiving, 2000. On New Year's Day, 2001, Taruk called and said that he was moving, but he needed to find a place to stay.

Three weeks later, he moved in with me, Jordan and one of my friends, Gina, who was temporarily renting a room with us. I didn't necessarily think that it was going to be permanent with Taruk at that point, but he needed a way to get out of that situation. And, obviously, I wanted him to get out of it.

Crazy? Sure, but when we were together, we just clicked so well. My instincts told me that he was a good man. I trusted him.

Our favorite hobby became those long hikes together. It was good exercise and, better yet, a great way to spend quality time and really get to know someone. You can learn so much about a person when it's just the two of you out walking, holding hands, for hours and hours. There are no distractions, just the two of you sharing your thoughts, feelings and dreams. Highly recommended for any couple, young or old.

I learned so much about Taruk this way. He told me all about his daughter, Tiffany. He was 23 and in rehab when she was born. Tiffany was living in Massachusetts with her mother, Tina, one of Taruk's former girlfriends.

Taruk also started to reveal some details about how he used drugs when he was younger, all the trouble he'd gotten into over the years, and his broken home. I had to give him credit for spilling his guts.

Women always want their men to open up and share their emotions. Well, you have to accept the bad stuff that comes out of it, too, I guess.

In Taruk's case, it was difficult to picture some of it because he had grown into an intelligent, clean-cut guy. He wasn't doing drugs when we met. We partied a little, but it was just typical social drinking. I didn't see his wild side. I only heard about it from him.

I was amazed by the lifestyle he was describing from his past. There was clearly a dark side there. He talked openly about his struggles. He was using words like "demons," almost as if they took him over at times.

My head was spinning from some of these stories. Looking back, they were red flags lined up one after another.

It didn't make sense to get involved with someone with that type of background, especially since I had a young son.

That's obvious to me now, but it wasn't back then because I just wasn't seeing that side of Taruk at all.

People do change. They grow up and mature. Just because someone made mistakes when they were young doesn't mean that should define them as adults. That's what I told myself and I believed it. Or maybe I was in denial. Probably a little of both.

He was confiding in me, really exposing himself with all these horror stories while we're hiking for hours on end. But, in reality, what we were living was more of an All-American lifestyle.

It turned into a risk/reward relationship for me. His past was a risk, no doubt about it. But I was living in the present and dreaming of our future. I decided the risk was worth it.

His stories were surreal. It was like reading a book about some stranger's life. He didn't seem anything like the out-of-control person from his younger days. He had gone to UC Berkeley and received a bachelor's degree in social science.

Even the troublemakers he used to hang out with had changed. JJ, his pseudo-brother who lived with Taruk and Hassan during some of the craziest times, was now an articulate college graduate.

Taruk was working at the Berkeley Youth Alternatives. He was a counselor, helping at-risk children. It was the perfect career for him.

He connected easily with most of the kids and was always concerned about trying to get them on the right track. He understood them well, no doubt because of his experience. He related to them that way.

At the same time, Taruk had turned himself around and could be a positive influence on them, even a role model. You could see how important that was to him to try to provide some stability for these troubled kids. To some, he became like a father figure, which was a source of pride to him. He really didn't have much of that himself growing up, because his dad was so out of control.

Our relationship was only continuing to grow. He said that it was totally different from anything he had experienced in a relationship before. I couldn't have been happier.

I was traveling with my job as an account executive in the hotel industry. He helped to take care of Jordan when I was out of town.

They got along terrifically. You really couldn't ask for anything better as far as that's concerned. They were like two young boys. I believe that they were thrilled when I left town.

Every Friday, they'd share a pizza and go to the movies together. Jordan's biological father had often broken his heart by making promises and never keeping them. Jordan needed a male influence and Taruk was providing that for him.

We went to Jordan's baseball games, soccer, and everything. I was "Team Mom" one year, coordinating the post-game snacks for the kids, running the snack bar, keeping all the parents informed of when and where the practices and games were going to be held. Taruk was one of the coaches and even ended up officiating one game.

Taruk also organized informal football games for the kids in the neighborhood. He helped Jordan with his spelling words and other school projects. He became that father figure, a mentor, just the opposite of what Taruk's father had been to him.

Jordan, meanwhile, thought Taruk was the greatest guy in the world. Jordan's friends felt the same way.

Taruk was a big, strong man, but he was just a teddy bear around the kids. They loved to climb on him and goof around. Taruk was a kid at heart. I loved that quality in him.

We had a lot in common, too. We were both high energy. We found out that we both played the flute in school. When we met, we were both driving the same car, a Nissan 300 ZX. We both loved football and outdoor sports, and we both had a passion for music.

One of my favorite memories is the night we listened to the CD from *Westside Story*. We agreed that it was one of the greatest soundtracks we'd ever heard.

We started dancing and sang to it from start to finish. We put together our own mini-performance for every single song.

At the end, I took a bow while he pretended to be the crowd, giving me a standing ovation. "Bravo! Bravo!" he exclaimed. Then he took a bow and I applauded for him.

We were in our own little fantasy world, and falling deeper and deeper in love every second.

Seriously, who does stuff like sing and dance to a CD in their living room all night long? But those are the kind of heartwarming things we did together. That's why I ignored all those warning signs and kept going. I had found the ideal man for me. I was certain of it.

Taruk's daughter, Tiffany, came to visit us for a while. She was a gorgeous girl, dark skinned with beautiful features and very pretty hair. She could be goofy, but sweet.

We took her to Disneyland and had a blast, going on every water ride and even a rollercoaster. Jordan and Tiffany were about the same age and would become pretty good friends. They really started to act like brother and sister, in a good way, minus the typical sibling bickering.

I could see some of Taruk in Tiffany's personality. She was a little hardheaded, shall we say, just like him.

Obviously, I was never going to be a mom to her the way Taruk was becoming a dad to Jordan, but it was good for all of us to spend some time together. I wanted to get to know her and get along well with her. That was another important step for Taruk and I as a couple.

Growing up in San Francisco, Taruk was a 49ers football fan when we first met. He even had a 49ers' "SF" logo tattooed on his chest.

Since moving to the Bay Area, though, I had become a maniac Oakland Raiders fan. You have to act a little nuts to be a true Raider.

49ers fans are the wimpy wine drinkers. Raiders fans are the hard-core bikers who dress up in black and silver, and try to look as mean and nasty as they can. It's Hell's Angels with shoulder pads, the best fans in football.

Not sure what that says about me - maybe subconsciously, I like the bad boy - but I was drawn to the Raider Nation.

This became a little bit of a conflict for us on football Sundays, because I wanted to go to the Oakland Coliseum to see my team, and Taruk wanted to go to Candlestick Park in San Francisco for his.

It wasn't easy. It took some serious sweet-talking, but I eventually converted him. He started wearing a Raiders jacket. It was a prime example of compromise in our relationship.

I give him credit. I'm not sure that I could have ever made that type of sacrifice myself. In fact, I know I wouldn't have done it. Turn my back on the Raiders? Not a chance.

We started going to a lot of the Raiders' games together. On a typical Sunday, we would wake up and watch Joel Osteen's church service on television. It's a non-denomination Christian service. Taruk and I didn't talk about religion a lot, but we felt spiritual and were drawn to Joel's upbeat personality and positive message.

After watching the 30-minute show, we might take a quick hike, then put on our silver-and-black gear and get ready for some football.

Usually after the games, we'd go back to the sports bar in a hotel where I used to work, near the stadium. We'd have a few drinks, watch some other NFL games, and talk with friends and other fans.

I still knew some of the people who worked there, including one of the security guards who was familiar with the ongoing issues that I'd had with Shane.

After another Raiders loss, we were drowning our sorrows when this security guard came up and warned us, "That crazy person is out there in the parking lot again."

Shane hadn't been stalking me as much lately, so it initially caught me off guard. I didn't think that he knew where I was living anymore. The thought of him trying to get back in my life made me panic. I felt like a trapped animal. I was terrified that it was all going to start up again. I just couldn't take it anymore.

As I was having flashbacks to all the run-ins with Shane, Taruk excused himself from the table, saying he had to go to the bathroom. I wasn't too thrilled with that, knowing Shane could come inside at any moment.

Taruk knew all about Shane. I'd told him the stories. He'd also seen some bruises on my arm from getting attacked by Shane one time. I was surprised that he would go to the men's room at that particular moment. He was gone for several minutes, which felt like hours to me.

When Taruk finally came back, he immediately said, "We really need to go."

I asked him why.

"We just really need to go," Taruk said.

It turned out that Taruk had gone out and approached Shane. They got into a fight and Taruk beat the heck out of him. Taruk was concerned that somebody might call the cops. He didn't need to get busted for an assault, not with his checkered past. So we flew out of there.

Shane made a few more threats later on that week, but that was all I heard from him until he sent me a short message on my Facebook page years later. I really think Taruk scared him off.

I was so grateful. Not that I wanted Taruk to go beat up all of my ex-boyfriends or anything, but this was different. This guy had been such a problem for me. He was always in the back of my mind, even on my best day. I always wondered when he might catch up with me again. It was frustrating and emotionally draining to spend so much time and energy worrying about how to avoid the guy.

But Shane was no longer a problem. Taruk had taken care of that.

It was a turning point, actually an exclamation point, in my feelings toward Taruk. I literally felt like he had saved me. Finally, it was over. No more Shane.

It was almost like, "Taruk, you are my savior."

It was still early in the dating process, but we were really getting along well and this took all of that to another level for me. We obviously had similar interests. We were both employed and making good money. We shared the responsibilities around the house. He was helping me raise my son.

And then he makes this statement that shows he's going to protect me and Jordan at all costs. That was huge.

The three of us continued to draw closer. Taruk and I weren't married yet, but to me, we were in the process of becoming a real family.

I did a lot of business in Las Vegas, so we decided to make a little vacation out of one of my trips. We stayed at a time share right on the strip. One evening, with the temperature well over 100 degrees, Jordan, Taruk and I had tickets for a show at the other end of the strip. We hopped on one of the busses that stops at all the big hotels - the Bellagio, Paris, MGM, you name it.

The driver went through the list of where he was headed and wanted to make sure that he hadn't missed anybody. "Is there anywhere else someone needs to go?" he asked.

Jordan, probably 7 or 8 at the time, raised his hand and blurted out, "Yeah, Toys R Us."

Everyone busted up laughing. It was hilarious. One of those great family moments, a story you'll tell over and over, like all moms do with their kids' most-memorable one-liners. We were making memories together and it felt so good, so right.

Taruk and I had talked about getting married. It was clearly the direction that we were headed. But I was still trying to get the divorce from my first marriage official. My ex wasn't making that easy.

So Taruk and I had no set timetable. We were just enjoying what we had as a couple and as a family.

We hadn't even discussed marriage in a while when Taruk called me one night and said, "Let's go to dinner." I'd had a long day at work and really didn't feel like going out. A pizza and a quiet night watching some TV on the couch would have been just fine by me. But Taruk insisted. He really wanted to get out. So I reluctantly agreed and told Taruk that I'd meet him and Jordan at Applebee's in about 45 minutes.

I was actually a little annoyed, to be honest, but I went along. I figured that he must have a serious craving for something on their menu.

We sat down in a booth and were just about ready to order. Taruk suddenly got very nervous, fidgety. It was strange for him.

He stood up and even bumped into a waiter. It was clumsy and a bit comical. I had no idea what he was up to, but then he got down on a knee and - much to my amazement - asked me to marry him. Jordan was right there at the table, watching everything.

I was totally shocked. Taruk told me that he loved me, loved Jordan and he wanted us to spend the rest of our lives together.

I was so happy. "Yes, yes, yes," I said, immediately.

I looked over to Jordan and could tell that something was wrong. He had this sourpuss facial expression. I couldn't understand why. It made no sense. He liked Taruk so much, but this obviously wasn't what he wanted. I really didn't know what was going on in that little kid's mind, but he was not happy.

Taruk picked up on it, too. He turned to Jordan and said, "I really want to marry your mom. We can be a real family."

Still the sourpuss look from Jordan.

Taruk paused for a moment, and then winked at me as he said to Jordan, "How about I take you to Toys R Us and buy you anything you want? Then will you be happy?"

Jordan looked up, the frown turned into a smile and he opened his arms for a hug.

"Dad!" Jordan said to Taruk.

Can you believe that? Great kid, but a little manipulative at his young age.

Off to Toys R Us we went, later that night, and never looked back. Despite his initial reaction, Jordan didn't have any problems with Taruk and I getting married.

We eventually exchanged vows in Las Vegas on Aug. 3, 2002, a little less than four years after Taruk and I first met. Jordan wasn't there for the actual ceremony, but we had a reception back in California at Berkeley Youth Alternatives, where Taruk worked.

Jordan made one of the most moving speeches that night. "It's about time," he told us. "I'm so glad that you got together. I'm so happy."

Jordan went on to say that he wanted to change his name to Jordan Ben-Ali. I was probably just grateful that he wasn't trying to negotiate another trip to the toy store, but this was an emotional moment for me.

I couldn't hold back the tears any longer. After a failed first marriage, and then that traumatic relationship, all my dreams for Jordan and I were finally coming true. I felt blessed. We were going to be a family for life.

Those hikes continued to be a big part of our time together. They were so rewarding, both mentally and physically. We got Jordan involved, too.

A typical hike lasted anywhere from three to four hours, unless we were in a hurry to get to a football game or somewhere. The trails were marked well with signs to show the length of the paths.

One morning, though, Taruk was feeling adventurous. "Let's try this," he said, pointing to an unmarked path. "It might be nine miles instead of eight, but it will be a little different scenery. It's one or two extra miles at the most."

My instincts said no.

"Are you sure?" I asked him.

"I'm positive," Taruk said. "I've been walking these trails since I was 13. Let's go, follow me."

Jordan had brought some food and water with him in a backpack. I had nothing because I decided that I didn't want to carry it.

Just before we left home, Jordan told me, "You should bring something."

Great son-to-mother advice. Too bad I didn't listen.

We got so lost that it was ridiculous. We walked all the way into Oakland, ended up near a freeway, and didn't know how to get back.

Jordan, of course, refused to share his food and water. He was sending me a message.

"Nope, I told you," he said.

I half expected to be sent to my room when we got home. Has an adult ever been grounded by a child?

We looked around on this seemingly deserted trail and couldn't see any civilization anywhere. I also couldn't see another person anywhere. We just kept walking and walking.

It took four hours of being completely lost before Taruk finally started to admit his error. "I'm not sure," he said, when I asked for the 10th time if he had any idea where we were. "I'm confused."

We literally stopped talking for hours. My feet were sore, my legs were tired. I was thirsty, hungry and exasperated.

Jordan got so cranky at one point that he sat down in the middle of the trail and refused to budge. He was boycotting our hike-gone-to-hell.

"I'm not walking anymore," Jordan said. "I'm done."

We ended up going more than 17 miles. We were gone for eight hours. It was getting dark by the time we got back home.

Perhaps, in the end, it was a little symbolic. That was the last time we hiked together, but it wasn't the last time Taruk would lead us down the wrong path.

# CHAPTER 3

It took meeting my parents for Taruk to fully realize what a dysfunctional childhood he had lived. It was one of those "ah-hah" moments in his life.

If all you've ever been around is an unstable environment, then how would you really know anything different? I guess he just assumed that his family life was somewhat normal, which was far from reality. He eventually recognized the insanity.

I was fortunate to be raised, for the most part, in a two-parent home. My mom and dad eventually divorced after I got to high school, but they had raised us the right way. They were good role models. They showed us structure and gave us stability. We were held accountable for our actions. They assigned us chores and we were expected to complete them on time. If not, there was punishment coming.

Education was heavily stressed because they wanted us to grow up, earn a good income and have quality adult lives. They pushed us to succeed through hard work. They acknowledged our achievements. Pride was instilled. There was open and honest communication. They guided us through tough times.

We were also exposed to positive activities outside of school. We ate dinner together and discussed our days. We went on trips. We attended concerts and sporting events.

Most of all, we were loved. My mom and dad did all these things, teaching us right from wrong, out of unconditional love for us. We were more important than anything else in the world to them.

That's how you're supposed to approach parenting, but not everyone is fortunate enough to have a mom and dad like I had growing up. Taruk certainly wasn't.

Back in 2001, we took a trip to Michigan to meet my parents. It was at a time when Taruk's father had been disrupting our relationship, like only he could do, and his mother was being very aloof and insincere like only she could do.

Taruk saw a completely different version of family life through my mom and dad. It was as if he grew up a Bundy and suddenly was a Huxtable. He was jealous. He wanted that type of love and support in his life.

Both of my parents welcomed him into the family even though we weren't married yet. They were not only supportive of us, but they showed genuine interest in him. They encouraged him to pursue a Master's in Social Work, because that was obviously important to him. They were looking out for me, of course, but they were looking out for him, too. Their encouragement was motivating to him.

During the visit, we talked about how we wanted to travel and see the world together. Before we left, my dad and step-mom, Mary, gifted us a trip to Hawaii at his time share. Taruk couldn't believe it. He wasn't used to that kind of caring and sharing in his family.

We were on the plane, headed back to California, when Taruk turned to me and said, "If I had your parents, I'd be President of the United States."

It was an emotional acknowledgement from him. It made me appreciate my mom and dad more than ever. I never looked at them the same. They weren't too hard on us; they were just perfect.

I felt bad for Taruk, though. Why did I get such good parents and why did he get such bad parents?

Some people actually believe that we choose our parents prior to conception. Whether you believe that or not, Taruk had life lessons to face and was expected to rise above them.

Still, it didn't seem fair.

I tried to put myself in his position. How would I have handled all that he went through? What type of person would I have become? Could I have overcome it?

The one story that kept popping up in my mind was from his 15th birthday party. We had talked about it many times during those long hikes. It was a day that would horribly change his life.

Taruk was a very meticulous person. His shoes needed to be shined, shirt and pants pressed. He made sure the color of his socks matched the pants. The knot in his tie had to be just perfect.

He wasn't a male diva per se, but he was well groomed. Appearances mattered to him, which was another quality that attracted me.

Besides, he always did his own laundry to make sure that when he wanted something, it was clean. He also did my laundry and Jordan's laundry, too, which earned him a lot of bonus points.

When there was a special occasion, Taruk took extra time to get ready. He stood in front of the mirror, making sure that his hair was in place and everything looked just right. It was all part of the excitement, the anticipation of a big night for him.

Some guys could care less what they look like when they go on a date, while the girls would agonize all day long over their outfits. It made me feel important that Taruk cared, too.

I can only imagine the anxiety that he was feeling as he got ready for his 15th birthday party. It was August 14, 1983, and that morning, his father had promised him a "good time and a big surprise."

"Something you'll never forget," Hassan stressed.

Taruk was so excited. Years later, he could still remember standing in the shower, pondering what the surprise could be. The band AC/DC was performing at the Oakland Coliseum. Maybe his dad had tickets.

Taruk loved going to the movies and pouring gobs of butter on his popcorn. That would be fine, too.

Or, better yet, perhaps his dad had organized a co-ed party. "Girls, girls, girls," Taruk thought to himself, smiling ear to ear.

What could it be? Maybe he wasn't thinking big enough. He was going to learn how to drive soon. Could it be a car?

No, that would make more sense for his 16th birthday when he was actually getting his license.

Maybe a trip somewhere? Aloha?

As he immaculately gelled his hair, Taruk decided that whatever it was, it was going to be a great time, maybe the night of his young life, because his dad had promised a birthday to remember.

Taruk spent almost an hour changing from outfit to outfit. OK, maybe he was a diva at times, even as a teenager. He finally settled on some 501 Levi Indigo Jeans, Nike Air Force 1 frosty white athletic shoes, and a red polo shirt, his favorite color.

From the moment that his dad delivered the birthday-party tease in the morning until nearly dinner time, the day had dragged on. The anticipation, the curiosity, made Taruk anxious, almost jittery.

Of course, that was part of the fun, too. The long wait for the big moment made it seem that much more special.

A few friends stopped by to play video games and listen to music to kill time. Hassan finally arrived around 6:30pm and announced that it was time to party. He gave Taruk a small package wrapped in newspaper.

Taruk immediately ripped it open and found the stunning surprise, something far from anything he'd ever considered.

It was a gram of cocaine.

For the big 1-5, Hassan Ben-Ali introduced his son to cocaine. Most parents light candles on a cake and sing "Happy Birthday." Hassan put a line of coke on the table and showed Taruk how to snort it.

For Taruk, it was the beginning of the end, like a down payment on his casket.

I won't ever get over hearing my late-husband share that incredible story. It makes me furious, leaves me heartbroken.

It's beyond anything I thought a parent could do. Give your kid cocaine? Really?

Seriously, who the hell does that?

Most of us can't sleep at night because we're so worried that our children might get caught up with the wrong crowd and end up doing drugs. You pray that some slimy drug dealer doesn't get to them when you're not watching.

But when you have a dad who's as crazy as Hassan Ben-Ali, who needs a drug dealer? Hassan, a dark-skinned man with a small build and close-set eyes, was the drug dealer.

Having heard this and seen the craziness in that family, I've come to believe that insanity is hereditary. No matter how smart, witty and handsome you are, a pathetic upbringing like that can come back to haunt you.

You can have a big smile and a bigger heart, but it doesn't mean that you will rise above it all. You can fight for a better life and still get knocked out in the end. Taruk Ben-Ali, my husband, was proof of it.

Taruk was born in San Francisco in 1968. I was 7 years old, living in Michigan, which was still healing from the race riots in Detroit a year earlier.

People all across the country were protesting the Vietnam War. Martin Luther King, Jr. and Robert F. Kennedy had been assassinated in recent months.

Taruk's mother, Sue Johnson, was young and wasn't ready to be a parent when she got pregnant. He grew up in sort of a hippie, flower-child atmosphere. Sue left him sitting on a blanket in a park for hours one time, while she was off doing who knows what.

Taruk's mischievousness was discovered at an early age. He was just a few years old when Sue received a phone call one morning, waking her up. On the other end of the line was Ollie, the owner of a corner store a couple of blocks down. Ollie informed her that Taruk had walked in with $200 and wanted to buy candy from him.

Good ol' Ollie gave Taruk some chocolates and let him keep the money. Ollie then watched Taruk closely until Sue came down to pick him up. She told this story often, chuckling each time over the grin on Taruk's face as they walked into the store. It was priceless.

She later realized that Taruk had taken the money right out of her wallet, which was fitting. Taruk did well for himself financially, but he still had a sense of entitlement when it came to his parents and money. He stayed in their pockets long after he became an adult. Perhaps, he felt that he had it coming after all they'd put him through.

Following that early-morning candy run, Hassan installed a lock at the top of their front door to keep his madcap kid from wandering off again. It didn't work for long. Taruk was too smart, too clever, and too resourceful. He actually dragged a chair downstairs one day, stood up on it, reached high and unlocked the door before heading off in search of his young buddy, Jeremy, who lived in the upstairs unit.

Taruk and Jeremy were inseparable. Taruk wanted his pal to meet the friendly woman who had given him a free donut at the corner baker. She thought he was a cute little kid and he sure loved her jelly donuts.

Jeremy's mother was the first to notice that the two boys had disappeared and immediately called Hassan and Sue. The parents all took off on foot in search of the dynamic donut-seeking duo. When they found the boys walking up the street, Taruk, with jelly on the side of his face, just flashed that adorable smile of his once again.

Taruk didn't take any money that time. He just relied on his charm to get what he wanted.

In fourth grade, Taruk decided that he wanted to play the flute at his elementary school. Sue found a hand-me-down at a reasonable price from a local music store that offered monthly payment plans. But before she had paid it off, Taruk lost the flute. His parents didn't want to buy him another one, so it appeared that his musical career was coming to an end before it really even got started.

That, of course, wasn't going to stop Taruk. He was a determined kid. If he wanted candy, then he dug into his mom's purse for some cash and took off for the candy store. If he wanted to see his friend, then he snuck out of the house and went to go get him.

This time, Taruk cut a deal with the music teacher to borrow a flute. Later on, one of Taruk's friends gave him a flute that she was no longer using. He stuck with it and ended up playing in the high-school band. Whatever Taruk wanted, he put his mind to it, and usually succeeded.

His parents eventually divorced and he bounced around, living with his mom, then his dad, then his grandmother, even an aunt, at various times. No structure, no stability, no accountability. He did what he wanted without repercussions.

After meeting Taruk, I thought he looked Mexican, but his mother was white and his father was black. Hassan's original name was actually Leroy Wright, but at some point before Taruk was born, he changed it to Hassan Ben-Ali and started acting as if he was Muslim.

Hassan's mother, Ruth Thompson, looked like an American Indian to me. She was married to a man named Wright, but apparently, cheated on him with a truck driver from Sudan, Africa. Hassan overheard a conversation one day and started believing that was his biological father.

I'm not sure Taruk knew what to believe. He was a little bit at a loss to find an identity. He often referred to blacks as "negroes" in a joking, but annoying manner.

I couldn't understand his attitude. He was black, but he didn't always want to admit it, which was all part of his father's influence from early on.

There was a private side of Taruk that could act a little superior to other people in certain settings. At the same time, he was helping kids build up their self-esteem, and race didn't matter at all. This was another one of the many contradictions that emerged over time.

It all came from his dad. Hassan tried to convince people that he was Arab. Who knows what effect it had on him as a child, growing up thinking that his biological father was some truck driver from another country whom he'd never met.

Hassan wanted to separate himself from African Americans, which is part of the reason he was never going to accept me, a black woman, as his daughter-in-law. I often cooked the so-called Negro foods, as he'd say. You know, mac 'n cheese, ribs and, lord forbid, fried chicken.

What's funny is how Hassan was right there, licking his lips, the first to clean his plate every time.

Hassan was a controlling, manipulating liar. Very superficial. He had to be in the middle of everything. He was disrespectful of women, never faithful, and would go around bragging about his sexual conquests.

He had tried to brainwash Taruk into believing that they had this Muslim background. For the most part, Taruk didn't buy it. Maybe he did early on because it's all he was told, but not once he was old enough to start making decisions for himself.

Taruk's grandmother, Hassan's mother, was one more walking conflict in Taruk's young life. She was known for guzzling a glass of beer and a shot of whiskey, "Boilermakers" as they're called, like a drunken sailor.

By the time I met Ruth, she was very old, living in a nursing home and unable to move, very frail. She looked like she had Indian blood to me. She was actually very sweet, a trait Taruk confirmed was generally not true when he was growing up.

Ruth, in fact, was mean to most people, but she loved Taruk. She totally spoiled him.

Unfortunately, she was another bad influence on him, more often than not. He wasn't even 10 years old when he witnessed a shooting for the first time. The person firing the gun was none other than his grandmother.

They had stopped to get gas, and somebody said or did something to upset Ruth - it didn't take much to set her off - and she started firing bullets all over the place. No one was injured. She either didn't have very good aim or was just trying to put some fear into someone.

Taruk couldn't remember all the details, but he definitely never forgot how frightened he was at the time.

This is the same lady who turned Taruk on to God. When she wasn't wreaking havoc, Ruth had a religious obsession, converting at one point from Lutheran to Catholic.

Her influence on Taruk didn't go over too well with Sue Johnson. Sue didn't believe in God at all.

So there was Taruk, with a mother who considered herself an atheist, a father who believed that he was a Muslim, and a grandmother who was a devote Christian on her good days. No wonder the boy was confused.

Taruk spent enough time around Ruth that he became a believer. He would bring home religious pamphlets and speak the gospel. Ruth, without Sue's permission, even had Taruk baptized. That's when he added Joseph as a middle name, becoming Taruk Joseph Ben-Ali. Joseph stuck with him for the rest of his life.

As he prepared for the sixth grade, Taruk insisted on transferring to Saint Ann's, a private Catholic school. They went to the school to interview with the nuns, but their application got rejected. Taruk believed that it was because his parents were divorced.

He was devastated. He couldn't understand the explanation. He wanted so badly, presumably because Ruth was pushing him, to attend Saint Ann's.

Ruth was eventually able to get him into another Catholic school, Saint Augustine, in Berkeley. She was literally trying to take over as the primary guardian. She even told people that Taruk was her son.

This all continued to irk Sue. Sue, an average-looking woman with mousey brown eyes and hair, had her own problems, though, and they ran deep. She was extremely opinionated, judgmental and downright rude. She was also an alcoholic and really didn't have much of a relationship with her son, anyway. At least not a healthy one.

As Taruk got older, his mom would try to compensate for her failures as a parent by giving him material things to make up for it. But they were never that close.

By age 13, Taruk was already telling friends and relatives that he wanted to go to college at USC, then to grad school, get married and have four children. That was his goal. He talked about it frequently, and I don't think that his mom, dad or grandmother was putting those words in his mouth.

He sounded like an awfully mature kid, especially considering the circumstances. I don't know how that was possible, given everything going on around him. He was acquiring some good habits somewhere, probably from a teacher at school.

Sometimes, kids mature at a rapid rate when they're forced to, when they have to be the adult because the parents are so immature themselves.

In some ways, Taruk became a normal teenager. He ended up at a public high school, Reardon High in San Francisco, after deciding that the Catholic-school route wasn't for him. He played football and was a state-champion wrestler. He graduated with impressive grades from a school that had a solid reputation.

These were encouraging signs, except for one counteractive development: By high school, he was living again with Hassan.

Living with his mom, his grandmother, or his aunt weren't exactly the most positive experiences, but it wasn't nearly as negative as getting back with Hassan. That was the evil of all evils.

When Hassan decided that it was time for him to step up to be a dad, he only stepped in as a buddy, and not a very good one.

Hassan's troubles were endless. He had many secrets in his life, including another son whom Taruk never met, and never knew existed.

Instead of guiding Taruk to do the right things to become a man, like a real dad, Hassan just wanted someone to hang out with and to be one of the guys. Maybe it was a mid-life crisis, but it was sad, strange and destructive.

Hassan ran what amounted to a frat house, using underage boys to create his own version of Animal House. They had what they considered to be "fun" on many nights. They partied together. It was a free-for-all at their home, basically a bachelor's pad.

JJ, a friend of Taruk's, lived with them for a while, too. Taruk and JJ called themselves brothers.

By this time, Hassan, a former postal worker, had acquired numerous properties through the years, including ownership of the apartment complex on Ashby Ave. in Berkeley, near the university campus. If run properly, it was a cash cow because of the location.

Hassan got his start as a landlord after inheriting his mom's home. He used that property to help purchase others.

But he was acting like Mr. Money Buckets and living well beyond his means. Hassan would give Taruk money for food or even drugs, and then just take off for days, presumably to stay with one of his lady friends.

Taruk was right behind him in the fast lane. If Taruk got in trouble, his dad always came to his rescue. Taruk got busted a few times for drunk driving, and even for evading the police. Hassan was always there to try to cover for him whenever possible. Taruk never faced any additional discipline from his dad.

They were both out of control. As if cocaine wasn't bad enough, a friend of Hassan's took Taruk a step further, showing him how to smoke heroine.

Taruk was high one night when he took his mom's car without permission, basically stole it. He got in an accident and smashed up her new BMW. He also got caught stealing beer. His mom wanted to make him spend the night in jail to teach him a lesson.

It didn't happen. Hassan went down and bailed his "buddy" out again.

Having his dad constantly protecting him like that was only going to work towards Taruk's long-term detriment. Any sane person should have recognized that much.

Taruk could do whatever he wanted, whenever he wanted, and seemingly get away with it. He was starting to feel invincible, kind of like Superman, which was dangerous with all the drugs and alcohol around.

Hassan was the worst. I think that he really started believing all his lies, because he told so many over the years.

Hassan strongly opposed his son ever marrying me, and he was vocal about it. After Taruk and I got engaged, Hassan wanted us to have a "spiritual wedding," not a real wedding.

Taruk mentioned his dad's idea while we were on a walk. I was dumbfounded.

"We don't have to get married," I told him. "But I'm not going to do some hokey-dokey séance wedding because it makes your daddy happy. We don't have to get married at all. You asked me. I didn't ask you, if it's come to that."

There was no argument. Taruk said simply, "Yeah, that is pretty lame. It's ridiculous."

In retrospect, the fact that he even brought it up was an indication that his father still had the potential to have control over him in a strange way, at certain times.

We went on with our plans for a normal wedding. Still, when I think back, it was amazing that his dad could convince him to even approach me with such a plan. But Hassan just had that type of power over his son.

Not always, not for everything, but just enough, on and off. He was that dangerous.

My divorce became official in July 2002. Taruk and I moved quickly and were ready to get married within a month.

Even on our wedding day, Hassan made a last-ditch plea to get Taruk to change his mind. His dad pulled him aside and wanted him to leave me, right there at the altar.

"She'll get home OK," Hassan told Taruk. "Her family is here."

The man was relentless, and much of it, oddly, was all because of that damn apartment building.

"She'll get the building," Hassan told Taruk shortly before our ceremony.

Taruk shook his head and told him, "She doesn't want the building."

It was all so weird.

Hassan feared that if Taruk and I got divorced - or if something happened to Taruk - I could take over part- or full-ownership.

I felt like telling Hassan, "Trust me, I can do much better than that apartment building."

It wasn't some landmark by any means. Some people probably think it's a dump.

But to Hassan, it was everything. He had lost all those other properties, one-by-one, because of his reckless spending habits, all to try to impress some young girls.

Hassan was on the verge of losing the Ashby building, too, when Taruk stepped in to bail him out.

When Taruk was in his mid-20's, he was badly injured on the job while working for Snapple as a delivery man. He opened up the latch in the back of the truck. The cargo wasn't secured properly and fell right on top of him. He got crushed by the load, suffered some broken bones and other injuries, and ended up receiving about $100,000 in a lawsuit settlement.

Taruk took about half of that money and bought the Ashby building, just when his dad was about to lose it to the bank. One of the stipulations was that his father could no longer be part of the ownership.

That didn't stop Hassan. He always acted like he still owned the place. He never came to grips with the fact that Taruk bought him out.

Taruk was still young, wild and mostly irresponsible at the time. His mom had to loan him money one year to help pay taxes. As a trade-off, Taruk gave her 18-percent ownership of the building. Several years later, when she was ill, Hassan talked her into signing away her part. It was always about the building with that man.

With Taruk working his regular job, he decided to let Hassan manage the apartments and let him live there for free.

Hassan was receiving social-security checks, which he shouldn't have been getting. He hired a health aide who was charging the state to take care of him because of his mental problems. He was crazy all right, but not in the way that they thought. It was a scam to give him income without working. That was his idea of a payday. He even received subsidized housing benefits. Just one scam after another.

One of Hassan's ex-girlfriends, Violet, shared an interesting story a few years ago about how they ultimately broke up. Violet was the only black woman Hassan ever dated. She was light skinned with green eyes. I thought Violet was the salt of the earth, a beautiful person inside and out.

They were in a club together one night and she went to the bathroom. When she came back, Hassan had his shirt off and was sitting in some guy's lap, yelling, "Yee-ha!" She said that Hassan looked at her as if to say, "You can leave now."

Violet did, and that was the end of their relationship.

Hassan tried to pretend that he was a real lady's man, but he clearly had this homosexual side, too. Ultimate confusion, which helped lead to his insanity.

Tina, Taruk's ex-girlfriend and the mother of his child, told me that Hassan once put a gun to her stomach when she was pregnant. He needed psychological help, but he had so many people fooled into thinking he was a friendly intellect.

Hassan often sat in a lawn chair in the driveway at the apartment building, wearing a Speedo swimsuit, reading books and talking to people as they walked by. Despite his oddities, Hassan came off to many as a smart guy. It was so fake, but those people were totally fooled. They hadn't seen his meltdowns. They didn't know the truth. They only knew one side: the imposter.

It didn't bother Taruk that his dad misrepresented himself as the owner. Taruk let it go because it made his dad feel good.

Besides, Taruk never thought that it was anything but an investment. He used to refer to the apartment building as, "The good, the bad and the creepy."

How ironic is that?

There were weird things going on all the time in that place. It was a madhouse. One guy ran a meth lab in his apartment. The walls were painted completely black. It took several thousand dollars to convert the apartment back to living standards again after he got busted.

The police department, at one point, made Ashby a regular stop in anticipation of trouble. It was just part of their rounds every night.

One woman had an alcohol and pill addiction. She was in her 40's and her dad was paying her rent. She had lived for a while with a guy named Henry, who had a metal plate in his head. I'm not making this stuff up.

This woman moved out and got her own apartment and wound up having an affair with a kid named Waldo. He was 18 or 19 at the time.

Waldo knew Hassan and Taruk. He even lived with us for a short time after Taruk and I were married. Jordan, my son, couldn't stand Waldo. Years later, we'd find out that my son's instincts were right on.

Taruk's parents were both part of the peculiar Ashby atmosphere. They both lived there, almost in earshot of each other. Hassan had a younger girlfriend, Hasira, although it didn't take much for him to cheat on her.

Meanwhile, Sue had remarried. Talk about awkward. How many people would choose to live right next to their ex?

When Taruk and I could keep his parents out of the picture, we were living the good life. But whenever they got involved, there was this darkness and craziness everywhere we turned.

Hassan never embraced his son's marriage, but he had to accept it on some level to try to stay on Taruk's good side. Unfortunately, I think that's when Hassan became even more neurotic.

Taruk and Hassan got into a fistfight after a barbecue at our house. One night, Taruk told Hassan to get out of his life, and if he didn't, he was going to throw him out of the apartment.

It was encouraging to see Taruk stand up to his dad on some of those issues, but I doubted that he could carry out his threats.

Hassan saw our happiness as stability for Taruk and felt threatened. He wanted to ruin our good thing.

Taruk would keep his dad at a distance for three or four weeks at a time. During that time, Taruk was happy; we were happy.

But eventually, Hassan would devise another scheme to get back in with Taruk. He would do something nice for me or plan a dinner for us.

Quite often, it worked. Taruk caved in.

He wasn't quite the same when his dad's presence was lurking. I should have recognized the potential long-term damage earlier. The warning signs were there, but I ignored them because I loved Taruk, and the problems disappeared when it was just us together.

Most of the time, that is.

Taruk had that tendency to make racist comments. It was so strange. I'm black, my son's black, he and his father, whether they wanted to admit it or not, were black.

But he couldn't totally let go of the brainwashing from his youth. I guess he really didn't understand who he was or where he came from.

I remember thinking, after he'd made one of those negative comments, "You're a damaged person. You're black, but you say that you're not. You have a past with your dad who was your friend but not really your dad."

We're a product of our environments and, in the end, Taruk was a mess, a tortured soul, because of his.

No one in his family looked out for anyone else. Not his grandmother, obviously not his dad and, to an extent, not even his mother. He was the only one who had any semblance of unselfishness.

His parents destroyed a beautiful soul. When he was away from them, he shined. His destiny was so much different than the final outcome.

He should have been president of some big company. Or even governor of California. Or, as he said, President of the United States.

He was intelligent and possessed leadership qualities. At least, one side of him was that way. That's the side I fell in love with.

He overcame so much to bring out that side. He just couldn't overcome it all.

I think he knew that he was worthy, but I don't know if he ever felt that he deserved true happiness.

His solution to any problem was always temporary, a quick fix. I guess it was inevitable that it would all fall apart for him, for me, for us.

# CHAPTER 4

About a year after we were married, Taruk decided to leave Berkeley Youth Alternatives (BYA) to take a job with an organization called First Place Fund.

As I look back, that's when everything started to change. It all happened so fast and furiously, in a matter of months. Our lives would never be the same.

I supported his move, even though I was totally against it at the time. I just had a bad feeling. It was a clear promotion on the surface, but that doesn't always mean better.

Taruk had it made at BYA. He was loved there. He was respected by staff, students and parents alike. He was featured in a newspaper article and interviewed on television, recognizing his contribution to the community. He didn't realize what he had at BYA, and he didn't fully appreciate it.

We'd become good friends with a lot of his co-workers. We tailgated at Raiders games with them.

Several had season tickets, just like we did, for years. Much of the management staff attended our wedding at the Las Vegas Hilton.

He was enjoying the job, too. It was fulfilling to him. He had a direct impact on young kids who badly needed help to stay on a positive track. There was not enough to do in the East Bay area for teens, which is why so many got involved with drugs or gangs.

The program that Taruk worked for offered many activities outside of the regular counseling. It had a little bit of everything. They traveled all over California for sports tournaments. There were music lessons - band, hip-hop, rock 'n roll, dance, drama, you name it. BYA was kind of a mini-YMCA. It also offered educational support for every class in school.

Taruk's bosses also helped him to finish up his master's degree on the side. They paid for his tuition and allowed him to leave two days a week to attend classes and study. I felt that he owed them some loyalty for the way they supported him.

But First Place Fund offered more money and a title change. That was his driving factor, misguided as it was. He was named Director of Child Services, a definite step up in his field.

To him, it sounded attractive and the title helped feed his ego. But he didn't consider all the possibilities.

If he had stayed at Berkeley Youth Alternatives, been a little more patient, he would have been considered for other higher-level positions once they became available. There just wasn't any way they could promote him at that time.

So he left all the security and trust that he'd built up over the years to take on what he considered a new challenge.

Sometimes, I think back and wonder if he might have been subconsciously sabotaging a good thing.

The new job quickly turned into a disaster for him. He was working with a group of about 10 people, mostly women. His personality and some of their personalities just weren't a good fit. He was chauvinistic and some of his off-the-cuff comments didn't go over too well.

He butted heads with several people. I remember going to a Christmas party in December 2003. You could sense some tension. A couple weeks later, Taruk was terminated.

He tried to go back to Berkeley Youth Alternatives, but they had already hired someone to replace him, and no other positions were available at the time. His former boss said that she'd let him know if anything opened up, although there was no indication that would happen anytime soon.

He was stuck, forced to do some soul searching along with his job searching. I didn't tell him, of course, but there was no one to blame but himself. He was paying the price for a poor career decision.

In some people, adversity brings out the best. They regroup and become more focused, knowing all that matters in the end is that you get up one more time than you get knocked down.

We all face adversity at different times, in different ways. There's no getting around it. It can be unexpected, a hurricane rips through your home and you have to start over, or you just gave birth to your third child and your husband is diagnosed with terminal cancer.

For most of us, the adversity hits much less dramatically, but it still takes strength to endure. If it's happening to you, there's no such thing as minor adversity. Each time you overcome it, though, you're better prepared to handle whatever comes the next time.

Or you should be.

Taruk wasn't. Adversity brought out the absolute worst, ugliest side imaginable in him.

I couldn't have anticipated that because I hadn't seen him face it before. We were living the honeymoon. Anybody can thrive when times are good. What are you made of in tough times? That's what separates successful people from the rest.

With Taruk, when things turned, it was sudden and harsh. He changed faster than Dr. Jekyll to Mr. Hyde.

Losing that job destroyed Taruk's confidence. All of a sudden, I was the only one bringing a weekly paycheck into our household. That wasn't bothering me, but he couldn't deal with it.

He could have taken money out of the apartment building. After all, it was his; he owned it. He should have dumped Hassan as the manager and started running it himself, but he didn't. He felt that he needed to help out his dad, who hadn't worked in years, if not decades.

Being unemployed soon became boring for Taruk, and there's nothing worse than boredom for someone with an addictive personality. A job where he helped other people was important, perhaps crucial, to his sanity. I think he needed that, and without it, he was lost.

I can't say that I even saw any of it coming, because it happened so quickly. He started to disappear for a couple of days at a time. I knew that he was hurting, but I didn't understand where he was going and why. I didn't understand the depth of his depression.

He'd told me about his past, but this was so out of character from anything I'd seen from him. I felt like I was suddenly married to someone I didn't even know.

He would call and not even make any sense with what he was saying. What I learned soon enough was that he was back on cocaine and heroin, and going on these little drug runs that usually lasted about three days. I really never thought that it was possible for him to return to that lifestyle. But he had. I was stunned, frozen.

His dad, not surprisingly, was giving him whatever cash he needed to buy the drugs. Instead of paying Taruk the monthly $4,000 profits from the building in a proper business fashion, such as a check to deposit in the bank, Hassan just doled out hundred-dollar bills whenever his son needed them.

I argued with Hassan, pleaded with him to stop giving Taruk money for that, but it fell on deaf ears.

Never had I envisioned him getting hooked on drugs again. He was in his 30's now. I assumed that he had outgrown it. I just didn't think that was him anymore. I thought that was the kid who got messed up before, not the mature man I knew now.

But as soon as he went back, it owned him again. I tried to approach him about it. "You have a master's degree and so much going for you," I told him. "Why would you do this to yourself again? Why would you do this to us?" But I couldn't reason with him.

Part of me wanted to be the understanding, compassionate wife and help my husband through his troubles. But a bigger part of me was a mom who didn't want her 11-year-old son exposed to any of this junk.

So I had mixed feelings. I wanted to hug Taruk and console him one minute, and then I wanted to slap him in the face, tell him to suck it up and control himself. There was a lot on the line here. His life, his career, our marriage, my son.

He had performed one of his disappearing acts one night when Hassan called and told me that I needed to pick up Taruk.

I was reluctant to get involved because I didn't know what I was getting into. The only thing I knew about crack and heroin was from watching television.

I was scared of the people who got involved in it, whether they were using or dealing. It was dark and frightening to me. I felt that anyone who tried those drugs had a death wish.

But this was my husband; I felt like I had to try to help.

Taruk was stumbling around in the parking lot when I pulled into the Ashby complex. As soon as I saw him, I knew it was trouble. His eyes were glazed, his shirt was torn and hanging out, his shoelaces untied. This was not the meticulous man I knew, even on his laziest day.

He hopped in the car and told me to drive him to Oakland. It was hard to understand what he was saying. His words were slurring. He was acting angry and bitter.

He gave me directions as I drove. As high and drunk as he was, he still knew exactly how to get wherever it was we were going. I knew that it was a place he must have been many times. His recall was uncanny under the circumstances.

Needless to say, I didn't want to do this. I wanted to turn around, take him home and have him sleep it off. But when I tried to talk him out of it, he snapped at me.

He showed me a needle that he was holding in his right hand. He claimed there was heroin on it and if I didn't take him where he wanted, he threatened to poke me with it.

I started shaking. I certainly wasn't going to mess around and provoke him. He was like a mad man.

"If you don't do this for me!" he screamed.

"OK, relax," I told him. "I'll take you there. Where are we going?"

I was a teenager in the late '70s and I went to Western Michigan, known as a party school. Like most people, I'd seen drugs, watched people getting high at parties.

But this was the first time in my life that I'd seen anyone so strung out on who knows what combination of crack, heroin and other substances.

He led me into a rough part of Oakland, one of the most crime-ridden cities in the country. I always avoided Oakland whenever possible. We'd cross into the city limits to see a Raiders game or go to a concert, but never anywhere near the neighborhood Taruk wanted to go.

We were somewhere in West Oakland, off 7th Street. He wanted - needed - drugs and this was apparently where he went to get them.

He told me to slow down as we passed what looked like an old warehouse. Most of the windows were busted out. There was trash strewn all over the sidewalk. A couple of husky guys with hoodies over their heads were hanging around a pay phone. They hung up just as someone walked by. It was, presumably, a drug deal in the making.

Over on the other side of the street were some hookers standing around. A limo slowed down next to them, a window was cracked open. There was a short conversation and then two of the hookers stepped inside the vehicle and took off.

It was all similar to the ghetto, drug-corner scenes you'd see in a movie.

Taruk told me to park the car, right there on the street. He grabbed the keys, got out and started walking down the street. I locked the car doors instantaneously. I know that I had a deer-in-headlights look as I watched him in the rearview mirror until he went out of sight. I wanted to strangle him.

Now what do I do? I was petrified. It was nearly 2 in the morning. There were no cops anywhere. All I saw were drug addicts, drug dealers and prostitutes.

I was careful not to look around for too long. I felt like a sitting duck there in my '98 black Nissan 300ZX sports car.

Was someone going to come over to try to break in? Was I going to get robbed, beaten up, raped, and killed?

I felt like I was in a version of Hell, sitting there all by myself, with absolutely no way out. I said every prayer I could think of over and over again.

I tried not to make any eye contact at all. I didn't want anyone to think that I was some undercover cop, or something.

Truthfully, I'm not sure how many people, if any, even noticed me. But I was so paranoid. I assumed that every criminal out there was coming to get me at any second. I curled up in the seat, still able to glance outside to an extent, while hoping no one could see me.

Taruk was gone for probably two or three hours. It felt like forever. All I did was keep looking at my watch. 3:17 a.m., 3:21, 3:24, 3:25 ...

How could Taruk have done this to me? How could he put my life in jeopardy like this?

All I thought about was what was going to happen to Jordan if I didn't survive.

I had no idea what was taking Taruk so long. Maybe he got attacked. Or was he just in some drug house getting wasted?

My head was turned toward the front of the car when I heard a pounding on the passenger-side window. My heart was about to explode.

I was so startled, scared to even look over. It was the moment I'd been dreading for a couple hours. My time was up. I was in trouble and had no clue how to get out of it.

Did they have a gun? Were they going to smash the window and come after me?

It's amazing how many thoughts can flash through your mind at a moment of extreme anxiety.

"Open the door. Let me in."

I knew the voice. It was Taruk.

In a way, I was relieved, grateful that it was him. But I was furious, too, and I had no idea how to deal with him in this condition.

I let him in. He fumbled around with the keys before handing them over. Thankfully, he hadn't lost them.

I started the engine and pulled out of there as fast as I could. We didn't say a word on the way home. He was wasted. I was bewildered.

Jordan was spending the night at a friend's house, which was a blessing. I don't know what I would have done. I didn't want him to see Taruk in this condition, that's for sure.

I certainly didn't want to be near Taruk, either, but I also didn't want another altercation, which I knew would happen if I tried to drop him off at his dad's.

It was a bizarre, eye-opening night. He ended up passing out on the floor, but woke up a few times to roll around and flap his arms while making some strange hyena-like noises. He was completely out of his mind.

When I talked to him the next day, he didn't remember anything. He couldn't believe that he had forced me to drive him to the drug house, threatened me with the needle, and left me there alone on the street.

This was the pattern that soon developed. He would be fine for a couple of weeks, everything would get back to normal, and then he'd disappear for a few days.

I came to realize that his drug use was an escape for him. As strong as he seemed on the outside, he was wounded inside to the core. When times got rough, he reverted to the only way he knew to deal with it, and that was cocaine and heroin.

He was so out of control at his dad's apartment one night that Hassan locked him up in an area we used to call "the bunker." It was downstairs near the office, a small room next to where he was ultimately found buried in the wall. Hassan left Taruk in this dark and dingy room to sober up and settle down.

I considered that a little cruel, albeit probably necessary. I called the police and had them take

Taruk out of there and send him to a nearby rehab clinic.

The clinic, however, would only take him for the weekend, which wasn't going to solve the problem for good. He had a couple of these short rehab stints. The therapists said he was a model student when he was in there. He not only took care of himself, he helped others, too. The staff spoke highly of him each time I went to pick him up.

Taruk would come back home and continue to recover for two or three weeks. He'd stay off drugs and I'd start believing that he would overcome it.

That's why his relapses were such a letdown, and so emotionally draining for me. You'd start hoping for the best, a full recovery, and then he'd just suddenly disappear again. It was on-again, off-again for a few months.

I was at work one morning when I got a call from the hospital saying that Taruk had been admitted overnight. I was worried and angry all at once.

His party binges had disrupted our family life, and now, they were affecting my work, too. I told my boss that I needed to check on Taruk in the hospital and rushed over.

A nurse informed me that police had found him literally half-naked in the street on Telegraph Ave. in another shady part of Oakland. He had been beaten up pretty bad. His keys and wallet were still in his pockets, but everything else, including his Rolex and other jewelry, were missing.

The medical staff told me that Taruk was so combative when he regained consciousness, they had to inject him with a drug to intentionally para-lyze him. It was the only way to control him. They feared for their safety, because he was so big and strong and acting so crazy. I thought back to the night when he forced me to drive to the drug house and couldn't blame them for how they handled it.

The police said it was as if he'd been left for dead in the street. He was barely able to verbalize my name and phone number to the nurse after he became coherent.

I found out the location where he had been picked up. I went there a couple of days later and discovered Taruk's car parked around the corner.

He spent about a week in the hospital, recovering. He never told me exactly what had happened. I don't believe he remembered.

This was creating quite a dilemma for me, because I had to keep lying to my son to cover for Taruk. It was an awful feeling, but what could I do?

I would tell Jordan that Taruk had a bad reaction to some medication, a horrible case of the flu, whatever I could come up with. I made up every lie in the book. I hated doing it, but I felt that I had to under the circumstances. If I had to do it over again, I'd handle that part the same way.

I didn't believe Taruk would ever harm my son, but I didn't want Jordan to see what was going on. I totally protected him from it. My gosh, he was only 11 years old. He'd heard about drugs, but what he knew was limited. He was a square. He had been totally sheltered. I didn't want him to be around it. He was too young to know the truth.

Who wants their childhood memories to consist of their dad being drugged up? Jordan considered Taruk to be his dad. They were tight. It wasn't until after Taruk's body was discovered that Jordan learned the whole story about the drug problems. By then, he was older and could better understand. I still believe that was the best way for me to handle an awful situation.

As soon as all this stuff started, my motherly instinct was to protect my child at all costs. That had to be the top priority, more important than what Taruk was going through. First and foremost, I had to find a way to make sure that my son wasn't hurt in any way.

I felt compassion for Taruk and his problems, but he was doing it all to himself. I felt disgust toward him, too, because his actions were taking a toll on our family and my career and ruining his life.

One of the toughest parts about the whole ordeal was that I went through it totally on my own. I didn't let any of my friends know what was going on. No one.

It was embarrassing to me. Even when I found him in the street, I didn't tell my mom the truth. My mom watches CSI. She would have had all kinds of theories. I didn't want her to know.

Taruk and I spent a lot of time with our neighbors, but they didn't even know what was going on in our lives. Taruk would take off when he was going on one of his binges. I was at least grateful for that part. Except for the one night after the scary trip to Oakland, he was never on drugs when he was around our home.

I guess I shouldn't have been so embarrassed to confide in others. I have good friends and good family. They could have and would have been supportive of me.

But I was ashamed. I couldn't admit it to them. I tried to hide everything and somehow stay focused enough to raise my son and keep my job.

My boss later told me, "I never knew you were going through all that. You always did your job. You never missed any assignments."

It wasn't easy. I was constantly dealing with customers. I had to put on two different faces.

When I was with Jordan or working, I had to be strong and hold it together. I had to forget everything that was going on with Taruk and be the best mom and the best employee I could be.

When I was alone, I just broke down.

My life was everything I'd hoped for when Taruk wasn't on drugs, which was actually most of the time.

But the relapses, however short they were, were exhausting and overwhelming.

I like to have a few drinks. We'd party at the football games. But this was taking it all to an insane level.

I was trying to raise my son. I was trying to earn a living.

I didn't know how to deal with Taruk. After he'd take some steps forward in rehab, his dad would be there waiting as his enabler again.

I had no idea how to fix the problem, but I knew it couldn't continue.

Tiffany, Taruk's daughter, came to visit in April, about three months after the relapses began. Taruk stayed clean while she was around and we had a wonderful time at Disneyland. Everything was fine. I kept hoping, kidding myself, that the worst was over.

About a month later, Taruk really threw me for a loop. He decided to take a week-long vacation to Mexico with, of all people, Hassan. It was so odd.

I was never invited. Taruk just told me one day, "I'm going to Mexico with my dad."

Taruk missed Jordan's birthday along with Mother's Day. It was totally out of character for him to do that to us. Those were special occasions. Nobody liked special occasions more than Taruk. He lived for them.

We didn't talk a single time for the whole week he was gone. He later explained that his phone wasn't working in Mexico. That didn't make sense in my opinion, but I let it go. It was the least of our concerns at that point.

Taruk showered Jordan and I with gifts after returning home. I just didn't know what to make of it.

It felt weird to have him back. His dad finally had him under his control for seven days straight. Even more dangerous, it came at such a vulnerable time for Taruk.

You can only imagine the brainwashing that Hassan attempted. I'm sure he outlined every reason that Taruk should leave me.

What Taruk needed right there was seven days of therapy, not a fajita-fest with Hassan. He needed to be around healthy people in a positive environment.

What he got was just the opposite - the negative vibes from a sick, sick man.

Taruk acted a little strange toward me for a while after the trip, even when he wasn't on drugs. He was more aloof, just different than I'd ever known him in healthy times.

There was one encouraging development during this time. Berkeley Youth Alternatives had a part-time opening.

I thought that might give him the lift he needed to totally pull out of this, but he wasn't ready. He didn't show up for work a couple of times. He was still irresponsible, consumed with the drug lifestyle and mentality.

He came drunk to one of Jordan's baseball games. He also ended up in the hospital again following another coke binge.

I went to visit him in the hospital for a little while. He wanted me to stay longer, but I said that I had to pick up Jordan.

Taruk called me the next day and said I had hurt his feelings by not staying.

I told him, "Don't you understand? My son is 11. You're a grown man doing this to yourself. I have a little kid and I'm his mother. I don't feel I have a choice. You do have a choice in what you're doing."

He needed long-term help, not just a few days at a quick-fix rehab clinic. I encouraged him to seek the necessary treatment, but it was one of those things where you can't make somebody do something they don't want to do. He had to be ready, and he wasn't there yet. I just kept praying that he'd get there before he lost everything.

I decided I had to stand my ground, but without totally giving up on him. It was sort of a one-on-one intervention.

"If you can't straighten yourself out," I told him, "you need to stay away from us until you can. I don't want you around us anymore until you can resolve your issues."

He got his act together and came home a few days later. The good times made me want to keep holding on. The bad times forced me to consider letting go.

I was torn. I wanted it to go away, or him to go away. One or the other. I couldn't keep living this lie and the rollercoaster of emotions.

We invited some of our neighbors over for a cookout one Saturday. I know the exact date: June 5, 2004.

It had been five months since these occasional relapses started up, but Taruk seemed to have had things under control over the previous few days.

We had a lot of fun getting together with this group. We would reserve the clubhouse and pick up a movie to watch on the big-screen TV. We went to concerts and comedy clubs with them. They were good people, good friends. I trusted them.

After we finished eating, someone came up with the idea of going to a popular night club in San Francisco. I didn't feel like going. It was too late to find someone to watch Jordan. Besides, I wanted to get up early Sunday morning to prepare for an upcoming trade show in Las Vegas. I told Taruk to go ahead without me.

I thought it was harmless. As far as I knew, nobody else in the group did drugs. They just liked to drink a little and have a good time.

I watched some TV, did a little reading and went to bed at around midnight. About an hour later, the phone rang. It was Taruk. He had driven his car and drank too much. He asked me to come to San Francisco to pick him up.

I told him that I couldn't. I didn't want to wake up Jordan.

Taruk didn't understand. He went off on a tangent about not getting carded at the club. He was 35 years old.

"I can't believe they didn't ask for my ID," he said. "Someone referred to me as an 'old guy.'"

I could tell that it seriously bothered him. He had become so sensitive in recent months. The dual life - psychotic when he was on drugs, loving and brilliant when he wasn't - had sapped his self-esteem.

I suggested that he take a cab home and worry about his car the next day.

He hung up, and I never saw him ever again.

volume 5 • issue 7 • July 2010

## Most Bizarre Claim Ever!?

*Title insurance policies insure 100 percent against forgery. If the insured party can prove documents in the transaction were forged, they are entitled to reimbursement of their losses. The problem is how to prove a forgery. In this case, the lender had the documented support of a police investigation.*

Liberty Title, a title agent for Lawyers Title Insurance Company, issued a loan policy on June 20, 2008 for $600,000 to JP Morgan Chase. Later, JP Morgan Chase was served with a Summons and Complaint: a Special Administrator had been appointed to the case (by the State of California) due to the suicide of the borrower who had no heirs to his estate. The Special Administrator filed a complaint with the courts to void the $600,000 mortgage, citing forgery.

The State of California determined the loan was a forgery based on a police investigation, which showed that on December 15, 2008, Hassan Ben-Ali committed suicide by shooting himself in the head. While the police were at the scene, the purported wife of Ben-Ali advised police that Ben-Ali was feeling guilty because four years ago (2004), Ben-Ali's son, Taruk, apparently overdosed and died in an Oakland motel room. Hassan retrieved his son's body, and took it back to the apartment building that was vested in his son's name. Ben-Ali wrapped his son's body in a clear plastic bag, then a blanket, then two tarps and placed it in a crypt. Ben-Ali then filled the crypt with dirt and sealed it by cementing a block wall around it in the apartment building's laundry room. Ben-Ali then assumed his son's identity, and on June 20, 2008 obtained a $600,000 mortgage against the apartment building. The proceeds of the loan were used to pay off an existing loan in the amount of $464,065.96 and the balance of the funds were given to Ben-Ali. Ben-Ali made the payments until he committed suicide and default occurred.

The Claims department agreed to permit JP Morgan Chase to enter into a settlement agreement with the Special Administrator while the claim was being processed. The settlement was to forfeit any claim over and above the $464,065.96 equitable subrogation figure.

In a nutshell, equitable subrogation occurs when the proceeds from one mortgagee's loan are utilized to satisfy the outstanding obligations under an earlier mortgage. Equitable subrogation affords the second mortgagee the right to be substituted into the position of the earlier mortgagee and afforded priority over subsequent liens and creditors – to the extent the loan satisfied the earlier debt. As a result, this claim cost the Company $135,934.04 (the difference between the prior mortgage and the new mortgage) – not the full amount of the new mortgage, which was $600,000.

While extremely bizarre, this claim provides our readers an inside look at how claims are negotiated to make the insured party whole without overcharging the Company.

# MACABRE DISCOVERY

**BERKELEY FIREFIGHTERS** remove a large container from an apartment building Thursday where police found a wooden coffin containing human remains Wednesday night. The coffin was hidden behind a false wall at the complex.

## Man's suicide leads police to entombed body

# The Grave Wall

Hassan Ben-Ali's holographic will.

Death Certificate of Taruk Ben-Ali.

## Alameda County Sheriff's Office
Gregory J. Ahern, Sheriff / Coroner
Coroner's Bureau, 480 4th Street, Oakland, CA 94607-3829
(510) 268-7300 / (510) 268-7333 (fax)

## Coroner Investigator's Report

**CALL INFO**

| NAME OF DECEASED (LAST, FIRST MIDDLE) | TENTATIVE ID | UNIDENTIFIED | CASE NUMBER |
|---|---|---|---|
| BEN-ALI, Taruk Joseph | ☐ | ☐ | 2008-03798 |

| REPORTED BY | REPORTED BY PHONE NO | REPORTING AGENCY | REFERENCE NUMBER |
|---|---|---|---|
| Emily MURPHY | (510) 981-5900 | Berkeley Police Department | 08-065141 |

| INVESTIGATOR | CALL DATE AND TIME | CASE TYPE |
|---|---|---|
| Philip Abrams | 12/17/2008 20:22 | Removal Case |

**DECEDENT**

| DATE AND TIME OF DEATH | DATE OF BIRTH | AGE | GENDER | RACE | MARITAL STATUS | VET? |
|---|---|---|---|---|---|---|
| FND 12/17/2008 17:00 | 8/14/1968 | 40 Years | Male | African-American | Married | |

| HGT | WGT | EYE COLOR | HAIR COLOR | OCCUPATION | EMPLOYER |
|---|---|---|---|---|---|
| 0 | 152 | Unknown | Unknown | Director | |

**Preliminary Summary**

Human bones found in a makeshift coffin that was buried in wall at the address of 2235 Ashby Ave. Possibly in 2004. John DOE may have been about 35 y/o at that time of death. DOE may be a black male identified as Taruk BEN-ALI. The father, Hassan BEN-ALI told a female friend Taruk BEN-ALI died of an overdose in an Oakland motel. The father took the body and buried him. Hassan BEN-ALI committed suicide on 12/15/08 (2008-03779). The homemade coffin was find by Berkeley PD during subsequent search.

| LOCATION OF DEATH | LOD TYPE |
|---|---|
| Unknown | Other |

| ADDRESS (STREET, CITY, STATE, ZIP) | COUNTY |
|---|---|
| Unknown  CA | Alameda |

**DEATH**

| Manner | Death Certificate Signed By: | T. Bartholomew #1035, Deputy Coroner |
|---|---|---|
| Could Not Be Determined | | |

| Cause A | Cause of death not determined by autopsy or toxicology (advanced decomposition) | Interval Unknown |
|---|---|---|
| Cause B | | Interval |
| Cause C | | Interval |
| Cause D | | Interval |

| Other Significant Conditions | |
|---|---|

**NOTIFICATION**

| LEGAL NEXT OF KIN | RELATIONSHIP | TELEPHONE NO |
|---|---|---|
| Wendy Ben-Ali | Spouse | (510) 303-5090 |

| NOTIFIED BY | METHOD | DATE AND TIME |
|---|---|---|
| | | |

| IDENTIFICATION METHOD | DATE AND TIME |
|---|---|
| | |

**INCIDENT**

| LOCATION OF INCIDENT | AT WORK |
|---|---|
| Possible Motel room ( still under investigation) | ☐ |

| ADDRESS (STREET, CITY, STATE, ZIP) | COUNTY | DATE AND TIME OF INCIDENT |
|---|---|---|
| | Alameda | |

| INVESTIGATING AGENCY | INV AGENCY PHONE NUMBER | OFFICER |
|---|---|---|
| Berkeley Police Department | | Sgt. SABINS |

**DISP**

| FUNERAL HOME | BODY RELEASED TO FUNERAL HOME ON |
|---|---|
| Smith & Witter Funeral Home | 12/27/2008   13:53 |

| Full Autopsy | Partial Autopsy | Inspection | Record Review | Inspection w/Specimen | EXAM BY |
|---|---|---|---|---|---|
| ☑ | ☐ | ☐ | ☐ | ☐ | Robert Zedelis |

Date Printed

**Alameda County Sheriff's Office**
**Gregory J. Ahern, Sheriff / Coroner**
Coroner's Bureau, 480 4th Street, Oakland, CA
94607-3829
(510) 268-7300 / (510) 268-7333 (fax)

The Berkeley Police Department began an investigation to this report from Nasira ███████. At 1700 hours, Wednesday, 12/16/08, the Berkeley PD went to the Ashby Avenue address and began an investigative dig in the laundry room area. While digging, a wood makeshift coffin in a homemade crypt was found. The BPD was able to determine that there were human bones inside the coffin. All police activity stopped and at 2000 hours the Coroner's Bureau was notified of the find.

Upon further investigation, I (ABRAMS) spoke to BPD Sgt SABINS, who said the mother of Taruk BEN-ALI, ███████████ told him that about 4 years ago, (estimated to be in 2004 but not yet confirmed as a positive time line) Hasssan BEN-ALI made a phone call to a woman identified as Cariena DESMOND-FAUCHER who is the biological mother of Taruk BEN-ALI's 16 year old daughter, Whitney BEN-ALI. Hassan BEN-ALI reportedly told he "Taruk has gotten involved with some bad people. He won't be contacting you anymore, but don't worry. I will continue to send you your child support".

Everyone that BPD has talked to has apparently said "about 4 years ago", is a good estimate, as the death occurred sometime in 2004. The time line has not yet been positively established.

It was reported that Taruk BEN-ALI, had an old major fracture of one of his ankles and had a skin graft. (PRA#493)

At 1900 hours, Monday, 12/22/08, I (ABRAMS) had phone contact with Wendy BEN-ALI. She said the last time she actually saw Taruk was June 6, 2008. The last time she spoke to Taruk on telephone was June 08, 2008. Wendy said she believes Taruk was at San Francisco general hospital when he had his leg almost severed and it was reattached. I called San Francisco general hospital medical records. No immediate records could be found on their computer system.

At 2030 hours, I had phone contact with a friend of the decedents, ████████████. He last saw Taruk in the summer of 2004. (PRA#493)

**Description of the Death/ Injury Scene:**

At 2158 hours, Wednesday, 12/17/08, Deputy WONG, Sgt. MCCOMAS and I (ABRAMS), arrived at the address of 2235 Ashby Avenue, in Berkeley, to make the removal of the decedent. Berkeley Police was on scene. Captain HART and Lt. JACOBSON arrived within an hour of our arrival.

Upon arrival, I went into the laundry area of the apartment building, which was on the first floor at the bottom of the south stairs of the building. Upon entering the laundry area, I saw a very short hallway to the right of the laundry room. In the hallway immediately to the left is a small room with a sink. In an area next to that, I saw that a small crypt had been made. Inside the crypt, in a standing position was a homemade coffin made of plywood. Inside the coffin in a fetal type position at the bottom was the remains of John DOE's body. The body was wrapped in a clear plastic bag, then a blanket, then two blue tarps. The crypt had been filled with dirt. Then the crypt was sealed up by a wall that was built around it. Across the small hallway was an office belonging to Hassan BEN-ALI.

Amount:        $20,000.00
Account:       175217543
Bank Number:   12100035

Sequence Number:  960646422
Capture Date:     08/01/2008
Check Number:     1543

Forged check by Hassan Ben-Ali
Example of many written over the 4 ½ years..

Capture Date: 06/17/2008 Sequence #: 860918300

TARUK JOSEPH BENALI
(510) 704-9883
2235 ASHBY AVE APT 201
BERKELEY, CA 94705

1522

11-35/1210
175

Date 17 ~~~

Pay to the
Order of _____ $ 5,000.00

Five Thousand _____ Dollars

**Bank of America**
Berkeley Main
2129 Shattuck Ave
Berkeley CA
510 649.6600

Customer Since 1997

For 01751 · 41147

⑈⑆⑈21000358⑈⑈1522⑈⑄1752⑈⑈⑈1754⑈⑊⑈ ⑈⑈0000500000⑈⑈

BANK OF AMERICA, NA SEC
▸1210003584 E2005 #1 84
06/17/08

0860918300

Credited To The Account Of
The Within Named Payee
Endorsement Guaranteed
Bank of America, N.A.

No Electronic Endorsements Found
No Payee Endorsements Found

Forged check by Hassan Ben-Ali
Example of many written over the 4 ½ years..

## EQUAL CREDIT OPPORTUNITY ACT

APPLICATION NO:

PROPERTY ADDRESS: 2235, Ashby Ave
Berkeley Ca. 94705

The Federal Equal Credit Opportunity Act prohibits creditors from discriminating against credit applicants on the basis of race, color, religion, national origin, sex, marital status, age (provided the applicant has the capacity to enter into a binding contract); because all or part of the applicant's income derives from any public assistance program; or because the applicant has in good faith exercised any right under the Consumer Credit Protection Act. The Federal Agency that administers compliance with this law concerning this company is the Federal Trade Commission, Pennsylvania and 6th Street N.W., Washington, DC 20580

We are required to disclose to you that you need not disclose income from alimony, child support or separate maintenance payment if you choose not to do so.

Having made this disclosure to you, we are permitted to inquire if any of the income shown on your application is derived from such a source and to consider the likelihood of consistent payment as we do with any income on which you are relying to qualify for the loan for which you are applying.

EXHIBIT #7
WIT: Wilburn
DATE: 5·10·09
PAMELA A. STIPIC, CSR

_____
(Applicant)    (Date)

_____
(Applicant)    (Date)

_____
(Applicant)    (Date)

_____
(Applicant)    (Date)

CALYX Form Ecos.hp 4/95

Taruk Ben-Ali's true signature.

45835

| DATE OF SALE | HOSTESS NAME | | X CUSTOMER SIGNATURE | | PHONE NO. | |
|---|---|---|---|---|---|---|
| QTY. | | DESCRIPTION | | | PRICE | AMOUNT |
| 1 | Cella-Stage | | | | 55.00 | 55.00 |
| 1 | Cleanser 3 in 1 | | | | 18.00 | 18.00 |
| | | | | | | |
| | | | | | | |
| | | | | | | |
| | | | | | | |
| | | Thanks! | | | SUBTOTAL | 73.00 |
| | | | | | SALES TAX | 6.20 |

For purchases totaling $25 or more, you, the buyer, may cancel this transaction at any time prior to midnight of the third business day after the date of this transaction. See the attached Notice of Cancellation Form for an explanation of this right.

**TOTAL** 79.20

By this order I invite the Independent Beauty Consultant to contact me via telephone, e-mail and/or U.S. mail for future beauty needs.

x _Mandy Waldman 510-461-715_
INDEPENDENT BEAUTY CONSULTANT NAME          NUMBER

THE ISSUER OF THE CARD IDENTIFIED ON THIS ITEM IS AUTHORIZED TO PAY THE AMOUNT SHOWN AS TOTAL UPON PROPER PRESENTATION. I PROMISE TO PAY SUCH TOTAL (TOGETHER WITH ANY OTHER CHARGES DUE THEREON) SUBJECT TO AND IN ACCORDANCE WITH THE AGREEMENT GOVERNING THE USE OF SUCH CARD.

**BEAUTY CONSULTANT COPY**

© 2002, 2004, 2005, 2006 Mary Kay Inc.   Printed in U.S.A.   10-010209

---

☐ YES! I'd love to be on your preferred customer mailing list.

| CITY | | STATE | ZIP | E-MAIL ADDRESS | | |
|---|---|---|---|---|---|---|
| | | | | X | | |
| DATE OF SALE | HOSTESS NAME | | X CUSTOMER SIGNATURE | | PHONE NO. | |
| QTY. | | DESCRIPTION | | | PRICE | AMOUNT |
| 1 | 3 in 1 Cleanser | | | | 18.00 | 18.00 |
| | | | | | | |
| | | 20% Discount | | | | |
| | | | | | | |
| | | | | | | |
| | | Thank you! | | | SUBTOTAL | 14.40 |
| | | | | | SALES TAX | 1.25 |

For purchases totaling $25 or more, you, the buyer, may cancel this transaction at any time prior to midnight of the third business day after the date of this transaction. See the attached Notice of Cancellation Form for an explanation of this right.

**TOTAL** 15.65

By this order I invite the Independent Beauty Consultant to contact me via telephone, e-mail and/or U.S. mail for future beauty needs.

x _Wendy Wilburn 510-461-715_
INDEPENDENT BEAUTY CONSULTANT NAME          NUMBER

THE ISSUER OF THE CARD IDENTIFIED ON THIS ITEM IS AUTHORIZED TO PAY THE AMOUNT SHOWN AS TOTAL UPON PROPER PRESENTATION. I PROMISE TO PAY SUCH TOTAL (TOGETHER WITH ANY OTHER CHARGES DUE THEREON) SUBJECT TO AND IN ACCORDANCE WITH THE AGREEMENT GOVERNING THE USE OF SUCH CARD.

**BEAUTY CONSULTANT COPY**

© 2002, 2004, 2005, 2006 Mary Kay Inc.   Printed in U.S.A.   10-010209

Wendy Wilburn's true signature.

IN WITNESS WHEREOF, I have hereunto set my hand at Oakland, California this August 16, 2002 in the presence of witnesses requested by me to act as such.

_____
TARUK BEN-ALI

The foregoing instrument, consisting of three (3) pages, including this one, was on the date thereof signed, published, and declared by TARUK BEN-ALI to be his Last Will and Testament, in our presence, and in the presence of each other, we have signed our names as Witnesses hereto.

WITNESSES:

_____
NAME

_____
NAME

_____ 2235 Ashby # 201 Berkeley Ca
ADDRESS

_____
ADDRESS

Fake will that was found hidden in the storage area of apartment complex-.

## Borrower Signature Authorization

**Privacy Act Notice:** This information is to be used by the agency collecting it or its assignees in determining whether you qualify as a prospective mortgagor under its program. It will not be disclosed outside the agency except as required and permitted by law. You do not have to provide this information, but if you do not your application for approval as a prospective mortgagor or borrower may be delayed or rejected. The information requested in this form is authorized by Title 38, USC, Chapter 37 (if VA), by 12 USC, Section 1701 et. seq. (if HUD/FHA); by 42 USC, Section 1452b (if HUD/CPD); and Title 42 USC, 1471 et. seq., or 7 USC, 1921 et. seq. (if USDA/FmHA).

**Part I - General Information**

| 1. Borrower  T∧ɾʊκ Ben-Ali | 2. Name and address of Lender/Broker  GRAND LAKE MORTGAGE CO  576 GRAND AVENUE  OAKLAND, CA 94610  TEL: 510-465-8206 FAX: 510-465-8203 |
|---|---|
| 3. Date      4. Loan Number | |

**Part II - Borrower Authorization**

I hereby authorize the Lender/Broker to verify my past and present employment earnings records, bank accounts, stock holdings, and any other asset balances that are needed to process my mortgage loan application. I further authorize the Lender/Broker to order a consumer credit report and verify other credit information, including past and present mortgage and landlord references. It is understood that a copy of this form will also serve as authorization.

The information the Lender/Broker obtains is only to be used in the processing of my application for a mortgage loan.

_____      _____
Borrower                             Date

EXHIBIT #9
WIT: Wilburn
DATE: 5·6·09
PAMELA A. STIPIC, CSR

Calyx Form - bsa.hp (10/98)

Taruk Ben-Ali's true signature.

Our wedding day, August 3rd, 2002.

Taruk and his father Hassan.

Family trip to Michigan 2003.

Taruk on our wedding day.

Jordan Smith giving us his blessing at
our wedding reception.

On our honeymoon Hawaii.

1ˢᵗ Anniversary August 3ʳᵈ, 2003

Our wedding toast.

Wedding reception.

Cutting the cake.

Berkeley, CA 2002.

Taruk the father figure and Jordan 2004.

Raider tailgate  Oakland Coliseum 2003.

Horseback Riding in Arizona 2001.

# CHAPTER 5

The traffic on Las Vegas Boulevard was backed up - isn't it always? - in the middle of another steamy afternoon in the desert.

It was Tuesday, June 8, 2004, and I was in a cab headed from my hotel to a trade show at the Convention Center.

Not that long ago, Taruk had talked seriously about uprooting to Vegas. He really liked it there. He thought Henderson, sort of a suburb to Sin City, would be an exciting place to live. Close to the action, but not too close.

We actually weren't big gamblers. If "whales" are high rollers, we were minnows. We put aside $25 as personal limits for our entire stay when we came, and we never won. But we were attracted to the energy that Vegas offered.

Most people only see the Strip when they fly in for a weekend of blackjack, sports books, free booze and showgirls.

But there's a considerably different side of Vegas on the outskirts, in smaller suburbs such as Henderson to the southeast and Summerlin to the northwest. You'll see neighborhoods with family homes just like anywhere else.

Except there are front yards without grass. It's all cement and rocks. Not too appealing to me, the girl from the Midwest.

I don't think I could have lived there. It gets way too hot for me.

They can talk about the "dry heat" all they want. I might be a dumb tourist, but I'm not that stupid. One hundred and ten degrees is 110 degrees, period. I just don't like to sweat that much. Matter of fact, I don't like to sweat at all.

I always thought back to when we got married in Vegas in 2002 and went for a "hike" on the Strip early one morning to get some exercise.

Taruk and I usually worked out separately during the week. He would go to the YMCA in the morning on his way to work. I would walk a five-mile loop around the Berkeley Marina after dropping Jordan off at school, or ride my stationary bike at home for an hour or so.

Typically, the only time we'd exercise together would be on our weekend hikes. During the week, there just weren't enough hours in the day by the time we got home from work, helped Jordan with his homework, ate dinner and watched a little TV before going to bed.

On vacation, it was different. We could exercise together every day. It was probably 6 o'clock one morning and we decided to take a walk on the famous Las Vegas Strip before it got too hot outside. We called it our "hike" and thought we could search out the best spots to check out later.

What we learned was that it gets hot a lot earlier than we anticipated. Try 6:15 a.m. We also found out that the Strip is an optical illusion. Everything appears closer than it is, much closer.

Our goal was to make it from the Flamingo to the Stratosphere. What were we thinking? It was the first time while hiking that I almost came to tears. Brides aren't supposed to cry.

We solved the potential heat-stroke problem by agreeing to attend a timeshare presentation, which didn't seem like a bad idea at the time. They offered air conditioning, a place to sit, not to mention food, beverage and tickets to a show.

We started off rolling our eyes, wishing the presentation would end soon. But all of a sudden, out of nowhere, Taruk's interest was sparked. He started asking all sorts of questions. I thought, "Uh-oh, I'm losing him."

They were great sales people who had a knack for creating need and urgency in something you just didn't need. Another grand illusion Vegas-style.

They knew that they had Taruk and they just reeled him in. He became hell-bent on buying one of those damn timeshares. While I tried to convince him that we didn't need it, they were doing a better job convincing him what a wonderful way to travel for free for the rest of our lives.

Free? They didn't include airfare, not to mention the $15,000 cost. Taruk fell for it. For the next two hours, we signed contracts and learned all about our new timeshare.

What started out as a healthy walk took a turn for the worse when we were offered donuts and a little shelter from the heat. We should have stayed at the hotel and paid to work out at the gym. That would have cost us about $14,980 less.

Instead, we were the proud owners of a timeshare in Las Vegas for one week a year. Terrific, we can come back to this intense heat for an annual vacation.

This is why they say there's a sucker born every minute. We were the suckers that day.

I shook my head as we walked out of there a few hours later, getting back into the 112-degree heat. We hopped on a bus and continued on our journey down the Strip, having been stripped of 15 grand.

Live here year-round? No thanks. The quarterly business trips to cover my territory in Nevada were enough of Las Vegas for me.

As I was complaining to the driver about that stupid timeshare incident, I noticed that my cell phone was ringing. It was Taruk.

I was so frustrated with him that I didn't know whether I should talk to him or not. He was supposed to watch Jordan while I was on this trip. But he had been missing again since going to the bar Saturday night. I came to the realization that I just couldn't rely on him anymore.

It was at the breaking point. I was starting to weigh my options, trying to figure out how - and if - I was going to end this relationship. My patience was coming to an end.

After a few rings, I decided to go ahead and answer. I had to address the issue with him at some point. Might as well get it over with. I was also curious about his state of mind. How severe of a drug run had he gone on this time? Was it normal or really crazed?

The first thing Taruk asked was, "Where's Jordan?" He sounded like he had a clear mind, which surprised me a little. I didn't ask, but I assumed that he must have been at home or possibly he had stopped by Jordan's school. He obviously couldn't find him.

Earlier that morning, I had dropped Jordan off with a girlfriend on my way out of town. Joanne's a trustworthy, dear friend who had agreed on short notice to take care of Jordan while I was gone for a few days.

Her son, Steven, was one of Jordan's best friends. Jordan would get to hang out with Steven and Steven's first cousins - Nestor ("Junior") and his sister Yvonne ("Cita"), who was three days older than Jordan and acted like "one of the boys."

They were Jordan's "play cousins." So Jordan was happy and in good hands.

Taruk, however, didn't know what I had done with Jordan. He was concerned and also feeling guilty for letting us down again. "I am so sorry," Taruk said. "I forgot."

He continued to apologize profusely for several minutes. It was the most sincere I'd heard him since the relapses had started back up in January.

I could tell that he was totally sober. I had heard his babbling after some of the other drug escapades. That's not the way it was this time at all. I was relieved that he was coherent and we could have a conversation.

It was a talk that would have a lasting impact on me and perhaps affect how I viewed Taruk for the rest of my life.

"I'm done with this," Taruk said, his voice quivering as he tried to fight back the emotions. "I'm done with the drugs. I'm done with the interference from my dad. I'm going to change. This is over. I am so sorry. I've really screwed up. What's been happening is in the past. As far as my dad goes, that's in the past. I married you because I love you. I love you. I love Jordan. I swear things are going to be different. I'm moving on with my life."

Wow, I had not seen any of that coming. I was so grateful that I took the call. One more ring and it would have gone to voicemail.

This was the most positive, energetic and confident that I'd heard Taruk in months.

To me, his words were pretty significant. Talk is cheap, but this seemed different to me, far more genuine than the other times when he was only full of excuses.

He finally was taking responsibility for his actions. He promised to get treatment. He was going to call that day about getting into a longer rehab program. He was going to find out about the drug version of Alcoholics Anonymous and start going to meetings. He vowed to work so hard at Berkeley Youth Alternatives that they'd eventually have to make him full-time again. He was even going to take back some of the financial duties of running the apartments from his father and handle it himself.

It was really a one-sided conversation. He talked nearly the entire time about how he was going to change and how he regretted what he had put me, Jordan and himself through. He even said that he wanted to call the Raiders about getting season tickets again. I just listened.

I told myself to slow down, to not set myself up for another disappointment, but I was so excited. I honestly believed it. More importantly, I believed that he believed it.

It felt so good to hear him talking about the future in a positive way, about how everything was going to get back to normal.

Maybe it was just what I wanted to hear. Maybe I was being naive. I know it's hard for people to trust that a drug user can change. They have a reputation for making promises and breaking them with the best. Taruk had done that many times in recent months, but he had also been a model citizen, husband and father before this five-month relapse.

On many nights, I had dreamed about getting that man back, and for Taruk to find peace for himself. I wanted to think that his problems were just a temporary slip-up. He had regressed into his old bad habits, but now he was going to fight back. He had never sounded this determined to fix what was wrong. He had not accepted all the blame before.

I think that I believed him more this time, too, because it really sounded like what *he* wanted, which is the most important thing to any recovery. He convinced me that he was sincere. He wanted to be a father to Jordan. He wanted to save our marriage. He wanted to get back to helping kids, so they didn't have to go through the struggles that he was going through.

You could tell he was scared of losing everything. I thought he finally realized that he was likely headed toward an early death if he didn't end this right now. In the past, I almost wondered if that's what he ultimately wanted, that he had a death wish from the "demons". But he was showing a strong will to live and a desire to live the right way. He had a huge ego. Death really couldn't happen to a Superman, could it?

I understood that I had to approach this carefully with him. I couldn't go back with blinders on and dismiss everything that had happened. On the other hand, I heard a man I loved saying that he was going to do everything in his power to change, to stay off drugs and to keep his father from being such a negative influence on us.

Taruk said that he still wanted to talk some more, but I had to get inside for the trade show. I was already running late. He said, "Call me back when you get done. I love you."

I said, "I love you, too."

Those were the last words we ever spoke to each other.

Several hours later, at around 7 or 8 at night, the show ended and I couldn't wait to hear Taruk's voice again. I wanted him to commit right there to a concrete plan for changing, and to put it into action immediately. Why waste a minute?

I immediately called him. No answer.

I called over and over again that night. No answer.

I called the next morning. Still no answer.

He never answered the phone again.

It made no sense. Why wasn't he answering? Where could he be?

If he had lost the phone, then he would have, I assumed, tried to contact me another way. But then I wondered if maybe he couldn't remember my number because it was just programmed and saved in his cell phone.

Given his recent track record, though, I really didn't know what to think. I couldn't help but fear that he had gone right back to partying, but that made no sense to me. That's not the way it worked with him. He would go on his little drug runs, but then he'd come back to his senses and he would be fine for weeks. For as long as I'd known him, he never went on back-to-back binges.

Was it possible? Sure. He had a drug problem. Anything was possible, but I decided that I was going to think positively.

To me, he sounded too good, too upbeat on the phone, to believe that he would hang up and go right back to shooting up. I did not believe that in my heart, nor in my head.

Of course, I wouldn't have blamed anyone else for doubting, based on the history. But no one was closer to the situation than me; no one heard the regret in his voice like I did that day. Was I too close? Did I believe what I wanted to believe? Maybe, but I didn't think so at the time. I was totally encouraged. I thought that he was ready to change and that he had a chance to pull it off. Otherwise, I was ready to end it.

When I continued to call and got no answer, I started to get a little more worried that perhaps something indeed was wrong. I just didn't know what it could be. I didn't know what to do.

I flew back to San Francisco on a Thursday, two days after I'd talked to Taruk from Vegas. When I arrived home, I could tell that he hadn't been there. It just didn't look like the house, his clothes, the bed, anything had been touched.

I immediately called his dad. "Have you heard from him?" I asked.

That's when the lies started up. Hassan, almost gleefully, didn't hesitate to inform me that Taruk had left me for good, that his son had decided to move on, didn't want the life with a wife and a kid anymore. "He had some kind of awakening and wanted to move on to a different path," Hassan told me.

I was speechless for about a minute, trying to process and make sense of what Taruk's dad was telling me. I didn't trust anything he said, but his words were all I had to go on at that point.

Taruk didn't want a wife or family? That's not what he had told me about 48 hours earlier.

"Really?" I said after Hassan had repeated the story for a second time. "We just talked two days ago. He said the exact opposite."

Hassan had no idea about the talk I had with Taruk while I was still in Las Vegas. That conversation was revealing. It was everything to me.

"You're telling me that, in a matter of hours, Taruk went from being of total sound mind and wanting to fix everything with me and Jordan, to wanting nothing to do with us at all?" I kept trying to pump Hassan for information. He certainly acted as if he had recently talked to Taruk and knew his whereabouts.

But as time went on, some of the details kept changing. That's just Hassan, the pathological liar. I didn't know what to believe and what not to believe. I asked Hassan whether he'd seen Taruk's beloved BMW. Hassan said that it was still in the parking lot.

That should have been a big red flag to me and a revealing clue. Taruk couldn't - and didn't - drive high, but also, he never would have left his BMW behind. It was his "baby."

My emotions were running the gamut. I had left California on Tuesday, about ready to give up on Taruk after he'd gone missing again. Later that day, I got a phone call that renewed my hope and faith in him and led me to think that we still might have a future.

And then two days later, he's nowhere to be found and I'm being told that he's left me for good and wants nothing to do with my son and I anymore.

What was even more frustrating was the only information I could get came from a man whom I had no respect for and couldn't trust. No one else knew anything. It was a total mystery to the rest of us.

I never filed a missing-person report with the police, because Hassan convinced me that he'd talked with Taruk. I didn't understand Hassan's story. I assumed he was lying about some of the details, but all along, I thought that they'd had contact.

If not, wouldn't Hassan immediately contact the police himself? I was giving him at least that much credit, albeit misguided and undeserved.

When Hassan told me his initial story, he didn't say exactly where his son had gone. But I felt fairly certain that Taruk wasn't staying with Hassan because no one around the apartment building had seen him, including his mother.

A couple of weeks later, Hassan changed some of the details, telling me that Taruk was being chased by the mob and had gone "underground" to save his life. "Those seedy people that he was associated with when he was in jail are after him," Hassan said.

Hassan calling someone else seedy? Now that was humorous. He said some thugs had come looking for Taruk at the apartment complex. I thought that was odd, because I'd never met any of these seedy characters before, and why would they show up in Berkeley? We had lived in Hayward for four years. Wouldn't they have looked for Taruk at our home first?

I never bought the mob story, not for a minute, but some of Hassan's details should have been another red flag for me.

Hassan's next version put Taruk in Arizona. I called some of Taruk's friends there, but they said that they hadn't seen or heard from him. I eventually started wondering if maybe he ended up in Las Vegas, where he had wanted us to move. Over the four-plus years that he was missing, whenever I was in Vegas on business, I looked around for him. I drove out to Henderson, just hoping for the proverbial needle-in-the-haystack. I also checked to see if he had gone there to get a divorce. I found out nothing.

Hassan's ever-changing storylines continued. Next was that Taruk fled the country and was staying in Mexico. Honestly, that one resonated with me for a while. Taruk said he really liked Mexico when he was there about a month before he went missing. I definitely thought he looked like he had some Mexican blood in him. I thought maybe that was a possibility. It made some sense, but I didn't know how to look for someone in Mexico.

I had called around to different states in the U.S., checking to see if he might have applied for a driver's license somewhere. No luck. I called jails and prisons. You never know. I was desperate, doing anything to find a tip that might lead me in the right direction.

My curiosity about Taruk's BMW wouldn't go away. A couple of weeks after Hassan told me that it was still in the parking lot, I talked to Taruk's mom and asked her if she'd seen it. She said it wasn't there.

I went back to Hassan for an explanation. "Where is his car?" I asked.

"I don't know where it is right now," Hassan answered. "I'll get back to you on it."

Yeah, right.

I had paid half of the down payment on that BMW. If Taruk left me, as Hassan claimed, I wanted to know where the car was that I partially owned.

Hassan wasn't going to give me any money back. I knew that for certain and just let it go.

I put together a list of all of Taruk's friends that I could think of, including one guy that he had met in jail. I called them all. Even the ex-con insisted that he hadn't heard from Taruk in years. I drove through some of those seedy areas in Oakland again, went past the drug house where he basically held me hostage that night, just wondering if I might see his car. I never went at night, of course, but I had to at least try looking during the day. My desire to find the truth, for better or worse, was growing in intensity.

With my search going nowhere, I talked to Sue at one point about hiring a private investigator to search for her son. Her reaction was so peculiar. She had no interest. I don't know if she didn't want to spend the money or what. But she never got involved in looking for Taruk at any time. I couldn't understand her lack of urgency.

This was her son. Didn't she want to find him? I didn't know if she was in denial or didn't care. It was a strange way to grieve for your missing son, your only child. I guess, through Hassan, she felt that she knew Taruk was OK, wherever he was, and there was nothing she could do about it. I gave her the benefit of the doubt, to some extent.

It wasn't quite as easy for me to handle this bizarre turn of events. Even after I vowed to move on without Taruk, my search for the truth never totally ended. I would put it aside, say I wasn't going to think about it anymore, but many days, it was still there in the back of my mind. How couldn't it have been?

In 2007, I called Violet, Hassan's former girlfriend, in Arizona. I'd heard Hassan was going to be visiting her soon. I was still thinking that Taruk might have migrated to Arizona because he had some connections there. I asked Violet, "Can you please ask Hassan where Taruk is?"

She asked him. Hassan's story at that point was that Taruk was in Mexico.

I grew so tired of the lies. I had personally stopped talking to Hassan about a month after Taruk went missing. I couldn't take the nonsense anymore.

Hassan had come over to my home one morning and tried to get me to sign divorce papers. He had the paperwork all ready. He said that Taruk wanted to divorce me. Hassan also wanted me to sell the timeshare and sign some healthcare papers in case Taruk needed medical attention. I did sign the healthcare papers.

I told Hassan, "If Taruk wants to get a divorce, he can come and tell me. I'm not going to get a divorce via you. I didn't marry you. I'm not divorcing you. Taruk doesn't have a problem communicating. You're going to be his spokesperson?"

I was enraged. Could Taruk seriously not have the guts to come to me? He sent Hassan, whom he knows I despise?

Just a few months earlier, Taruk had insisted that I legally change my last name from Wilburn to Ben-Ali. I hadn't done it previously because of 9/11.

The only time I ever signed my name Wendy Ben-Ali was when we bought the timeshare together in Las Vegas the weekend we got married. Outside of that, I always went by Wilburn.

We had agreed that taking on the Arab name wouldn't be a wise move under the circumstances, especially in my industry. The company I worked for was based in France. I spent a lot of time dealing with CEOs.

But by 2004, things had calmed down somewhat in the aftermath of 9/11 and we decided that I would go ahead and make the name change.

Jordan had already adopted Ben-Ali, because he considered Taruk to be his dad. Taruk wanted to officially adopt Jordan, but I said no, out of undeserving respect for his biological father. Since I chose not to allow the adoption, Taruk insisted that I at least make Jordan's biological dad pay child support, which he had not done since we left him in 1996, eight years earlier.

Taruk, when he was off drugs and healthy, really wanted us all to have the same name. He checked into the requirements and found out that I had to go through the Las Vegas courts to make the change official, because that's where we were married.

About two weeks after Taruk disappeared, the paperwork I needed finally arrived in the mail. I broke down in tears when I opened the letter.

Now, just weeks later, his father was telling me to sign divorce papers. If he could have read my mind, Hassan would have known I wanted him to take those papers and shove them you know where. There was no way I was signing anything unless Taruk talked to me face-to-face. Absolutely no way was I going to accept some coward approach to a divorce.

I wanted Taruk to come to me and explain why he would abandon my son and me. He was going to have to step up and be a man about this if he wanted a divorce.

I was waiting for that to happen somehow, someway, someday. I thought, eventually, he'd show up. He had to. Otherwise, he wasn't getting the divorce.

All along, our friends were adamant that Taruk hadn't just flat out left me. But they saw the best of our relationship. They called us "The Super Couple."

Taruk once told the guys that if I wasn't invited to go wherever they were going, he wasn't going because I was his "best friend." So we all started to occasionally travel as couples and constantly hung out as couples. There were five couples in all, with everyone living in the same complex.

None of them could understand what happened to Taruk. They just didn't believe that he dumped me like Hassan was saying. Of course, these friends didn't know the whole story because Taruk and I, amazingly enough, had hidden all his drug problems from them.

Even if no one else could believe that Taruk had really left me, I had to, at some point, come to terms with that possibility, if only for my own sanity in trying to move forward. I felt I had no other choice. I had to almost try to convince myself to believe it, just to have any chance of going on with my life.

Part of me was angry. Even if I couldn't totally believe that he left, I knew something had happened. There had to be some explanation. I didn't think he was hiding from the mob or buried in some wall, that's for sure.

I was exasperated. I didn't know what to think. That was the toughest part. One day, I thought one thing; the next day, I thought something completely different.

I should have gone to therapy right there, but I didn't. I told myself that I was a strong person and I'd deal with it. But it was wearing me out.

I was guilt-ridden at times. I wondered what I could have or should have done differently. Did I cause some of this? How much of it was my fault? Did my ambivalence lead to it? Should we have been partying at those football games? Could that have contributed to his relapse?

So many thoughts run through your mind when you don't have any answers. Some are legitimate thoughts, some not. I knew that it wasn't fair to blame myself. This was on him, not me. But I still found ways to try to put the blame on myself, at times.

I was mad at him one day, mad at myself the next day, mad at his dad every day.

I started down the wrong road with some destructive behavior myself. I'd get home from work, and after putting Jordan to bed, I'd start drinking. It was the best way to temporarily wipe away the pain.

My son had to call 911 one night. I ended up in the hospital for a short period of time. It was a wake-up call. I knew I had to stop. My biggest fear:

What would happen to Jordan if something happened to me?

The excessive drinking didn't last long. Jordan was incentive enough to put an end to it. But it was a little scary while it lasted.

That incident with the 911 call led me to realize that blaming myself wasn't the answer. I had to start going to therapy, which helped to sort out some of my conflicting feelings. I couldn't feel sorry for myself. That wasn't going to bring Taruk back and keep him off of drugs.

I kept telling myself, "I didn't do this. I didn't create this problem."

I had to come to terms with that part, but it took time. You'll never guess who helped me the most. It was my son, 11-year-old Jordan.

He could see the agony I was going through. I was in my bedroom, crying one night, when he approached me. "OK, Mom, we're going to give him three more weeks to come back," Jordan said. "If he doesn't come back, Mom, we're going to let it go. We're not going to talk about him anymore. If he doesn't care about us, then we can't care about him."

I don't know where he found the insight at such a young age, but his point hit home. Jordan was being the strong one; I was the weak one.

Jordan is a Taurus. He's really practical. I'm not like that. He's more cut and dried than I am. There's no gray area with him. That's just who he is.

I have no doubt that Jordan was hurting just as badly as I was. But he kept the pain to himself. He was trying to protect me. He knew that if he broke down, that would only make me more of a mess.

He became an adult quickly through all of this turmoil. He suppressed his feelings so I wouldn't fall apart. And, the truth is, I think it really did keep me from falling apart.

When those three weeks were up, I took down all of the pictures with Taruk in them. Jordan and I tried to move forward and put it all behind us. But I simply had to get out of that home. Every time I walked into a room, all I could think of was, "That's the wall we painted together. That's the photo from our honeymoon in Hawaii. That's ..."

All of our good times, all of our family times, Christmas, Jordan's birthday parties, our barbecues, dancing together to Westside Story, everything was in there. Every time I came home, I wondered, "Is he going to be here?" And every time, I was disappointed when I opened the door and he wasn't.

I had to get out of that place. We had to get out of there. The energy in the home was devastating.

I asked Hassan to come and pick up Taruk's things. We moved into another townhouse in the same community. I still wanted to be close to our friends, but it had to be a different unit with a different view, different colors on the walls, some new furniture. It couldn't remind me of Taruk everywhere I looked.

That Labor Day, I invited a lot of family over for a barbecue. It was kind of a housewarming. Taruk's mom came, too, which was a mistake. She started to get emotional. "This is a beautiful place," Sue said. "I can't believe he's not here to enjoy this."

Oddly, that was also the only time I ever saw her get emotional about Taruk. I tried to get her to stop. I had already cried all I could cry at that point. Once I moved, that was going to be it for me. I wasn't going to mope. I wasn't going to take everything, all the bad energy, to the new home. At least, that's what I told myself.

In reality, I still thought about Taruk. I know Jordan did, too. He had to be distraught over losing his father figure, whether he showed it or not. It probably didn't help him to hold it all inside.

After we got into our new place, Jordan and I didn't discuss Taruk much. Kids are pretty good about living in the present. They don't dwell on the past and look so far into the future as much as adults do.

Taruk and I had had all kinds of dreams for the future. The last time I heard his voice, we discussed some of those dreams. I thought Taruk and I were going to be together forever. I was certain of it.

But I had to take my son's advice. I had to try to move on. What made it so difficult, what I ultimately kept coming back to, was that last conversation I had with Taruk. If we didn't have that talk and he just took off, my whole approach would have been different.

Based on that conversation, there was no way he left me like that, right? I had such a hard time accepting that he could have done that after talking to him.

But then there was that other voice in my head, which was telling me, "How long are you going to sit here obsessing about one conversation? That's stupid. You're not making any sense. What about all those times he let you down? What about the heroin needle he threatened you with? Get a clue. He isn't calling you. He isn't coming back. Face it."

It would have been different had I known that he was dead. The sadness would have been there, but it would have been a different kind of emotion. The kind of sadness that I had was down to the thought that he had abandoned me; he intentionally hurt me and didn't have the guts to give an explanation.

There were times when I stepped back and said to myself, "You know, considering all the drug problems, it's probably better for Jordan and I that Taruk isn't in our lives anymore."

It was inevitable that would cross my mind - "We're better off this way" - but my emotions still continued to flip-flop constantly. Naturally, there was that part of me thinking maybe this was for the best, that Taruk needed to live this type of life without hurting Jordan and I. If that's the way it was going to be, on and off drugs all the time, I absolutely didn't need it, didn't want him under those circumstances.

But that last call seriously messed with my head and my emotions. It left so much unanswered for me. If he had called back a week later and said he changed his mind and didn't want the family life, as Hassan suggested, that would have still hurt, but I could have accepted it in time. I could have legitimately moved on a lot easier.

It's clear to me now that Taruk had way too much to say to ever be silenced, and he was silent at the end. That wasn't Taruk. He was a communicator.

I knew that deep inside, but I was angry. I didn't want to be naive. I wanted answers. But there were no answers to be found. I said to myself in frustration, "This is what you leave me with, Taruk? You say all of that, and then disappear off the face of the Earth?"

# CHAPTER 6

December has always been my favorite time of the year. The spirit of Santa Claus runs deep. I love to put up decorations and sing Christmas carols, but the best part is just seeing the joy of people in the giving mood.

My birthday is also in December, on the 12th. Some people wouldn't like that because your birthday can get lost in the holiday season, but I love it. A full month of celebrating - from putting my tree up the day after Thanksgiving, to my birthday, to Christmas Eve and Christmas Day, to New Year's Eve and New Year's Day. No wonder health clubs are packed in January, with everyone trying to give back what they gained.

Many years ago, I started a tradition of hosting a holiday party at my home the Friday before Christmas. All of my close friends and their kids would be invited. I would buy gifts for everyone. It's an opportunity for me to show how much my friends mean to me. I would start looking forward to that day several weeks ahead of time.

How I felt about this wonderful time of the year, however, was never quite the same after Monday, December 15, 2008, a day that would trigger a series of events that would change my life forever.

I had just turned 47 three days earlier and was busy organizing the Christmas party for later in the week. My life was a mess in many ways, but getting ready for the party helped to make the problems temporarily disappear. Giving does wonders for your soul. To see my friends' kids open those presents made me feel so good inside.

I was home preparing the menu, which always features fried chicken wings, greens, catfish nuggets, mac 'n cheese, cornbread, autumn cake, and last but not least, my "Expensive Cookies." The cookies, a combination of chocolate chips, oatmeal and nuts, were a special recipe that I'd gotten a couple of years earlier from a girlfriend in Atlanta, originally made famous by Neiman-Marcus. I send them as gifts via mail every year and receive year-round requests to send more. But I only make them at Christmas. While they taste incredible, they're also very time-consuming.

One of my favorite holiday songs, "I'm Dreaming of a White Christmas" was playing on the stereo as I hustled around the kitchen, but the wonderful spirit I was feeling was about to be quickly sapped from me.

I'm not proud of how I responded, but I couldn't help it. I don't mean to be cold or indifferent. I'm usually the first in tears at a funeral or even when I hear a sad story about a complete stranger. This was an unusual circumstance, though.

The phone call came from Sue Johnson in the middle of the evening. She informed me that Hassan, who was 60 years old, had committed suicide. Sue was completely heartbroken. "He was my best friend," she said, breaking down in tears. I did try to console her, to the best of my abilities, but I wasn't feeling the same type of pain.

Taruk's parents had been divorced for many years. She had been remarried to a man named Brad Johnson, but they still lived in the same apartment building as Hassan, one level below her ex-husband.

While Sue was so distraught, I felt absolutely nothing. I was completely ambivalent, no emotion, certainly not any sympathy. I wasn't going to shed a tear over Hassan Ben-Ali, the snake who had given his son cocaine at age 15 and had threatened to kill me in the past.

I didn't go around singing, "Ding, dong, the wicked man is dead," but I wasn't going to lose any sleep over it, that's for darned sure. He was so fake. I thought back to the hikes that he took with Taruk and I, as a way to try to befriend me. Why? Because he was losing his grip on Taruk, that's why. I never bought any of it. He wasn't pleasant to me and now he was dead. Sorry, I did not feel bad about it.

Some details of the suicide started to trickle out in the next day's newspaper. Police had responded to 2235 Ashby Avenue around 6 p.m. after receiving calls about an argument, according to the Oakland Tribune. When they arrived, Hassan was by himself inside of the apartment.

"The man turned away from police officers and fatally shot himself in the head with a handgun," the Tribune reported. "The Berkeley Fire Department took (Hassan) to Highland Hospital in Oakland, where he was pronounced dead."

Taruk had been missing for about 4 1/2 years at this point. It wasn't the first suicide of someone close to him. One of his best friends had also taken his life several years earlier. We had talked about his friend several times. Taruk was angry about it. He thought his friend should have been stronger and not just given up like he did.

As for Hassan, I hadn't spoken with him in years. Jordan was now 15 years old and we had moved on with our lives. Hassan's death and listening to Sue's reaction only brought back a lot of bad memories and ill feelings. I really didn't need those negative vibes back in my life.

Over the next couple of days, there were more stories about Hassan and rumors started flying.

The Oakland Tribune interviewed a couple of his neighbors. "He was the kind of person who would always say, 'Hi,'" Crystal Haviland, who lived next door to the apartment building, told the Tribune. "He was a presence in the neighborhood."

Another neighbor, Rosemary Northcraft, told the paper that Hassan "seemed well-educated and reasonable. He must have had something tremendous weighing on his mind." While I couldn't feel emotional about Hassan's death, the idea of a person taking their own life is so incredibly sad. My girlfriend's son hung himself when he was 15 years old. It absolutely destroyed her. She blamed herself. We cried many times together. If that had been Jordan, I wouldn't have wanted to live another day. It would have killed me for sure. I would have felt that I had no reason to live. So I could understand her pain.

But you have to find a way to keep going, no matter what happens in life. My feeling is that suicide is for very wounded people, those who can't or won't take responsibility for their lives and their actions. They are in complete despair. I know that Taruk felt the same way about it. We both believed that suicide is a sin, although I do feel for that kind of pain, where you no longer see the light at the end of the tunnel. That's heartbreaking.

In the aftermath of Hassan's death, the speculation became more and more rampant, none of which I initially believed. All I was getting at the time was second-hand information from Taruk's mother. The rumor, according to Sue, was that one of Hassan's girlfriends, Hasira, had given police a tip about a dead body being hidden in the apartment building.

Obviously, the first thought was Taruk. But I immediately dismissed it. I thought Hasira was about as reliable as a Michigan weather forecast. She was just a kook who had a disturbing imagination and peculiar beliefs.

Never in my wildest dreams did I think the police, of all people, would ever consider her story credible enough to start searching the building. "It's insane. They're never going to believe this," I told Sue Johnson.

Wow, was I wrong.

Whatever Hasira told police, it was compelling. Within around 48 hours, a week before Christmas, they hauled shovels into that building and broke down the wall. I was floored. I immediately wondered how Hasira had gotten that out of Hassan and how long had she known?

It wasn't until the next morning that the news broke. I was devastated, standing there, watching on television as my husband's remains were carried out of the building in a homemade coffin.

When Sue called me that morning, while I was driving home from my coffee run, I suspected that whatever they were showing on the newscast involved Hassan and/or Taruk, but I never, never, never envisioned anything quite like what I saw.

Hasira's unfathomable story had been true. I watched in utter disbelief, weeping uncontrollably, as I started to find out what had really happened to my husband.

Jordan's words, "My dad is really dead," will ring in my ears for as long as I live.

I will also never forget some unexplainable and unforgivable comments from Taruk's mother. People have different ways of coping with death, but hers made no sense.

She was upset that Hasira had told police about the body. "I don't know why she didn't just keep her mouth shut," Sue said.

I shook my head and asked, "Why would you want her to do that?"

For a mother who had just found out that her only son, missing for years, had been found dead, buried in a wall in the same building where she lived, right under her nose, the reaction was so incredibly peculiar.

Who put him there? I was coming to the realization that it had to be Hassan. The guilt was what led to his suicide.

I kept asking myself over and over, "How could any father ever do that to his son?"

I needed someone to talk to, someone to cry with, and someone to help me sort through all the madness.

The person I turned to was my friend Gina, who was living with me when I first met Taruk. Our friendship had gone through some rocky times, but I needed her more than ever.

Gina and I had a lot in common. We had worked together, I even trained her, and we were both single parents. We lived together at two different residences and helped to raise each other's children.

She felt uncomfortable when Taruk moved in. I can't blame her. We needed her room for Jordan, who had been staying in my room. The apartment was in my name and I pulled rank on her. That's the way it goes sometimes.

It led to a major blow-up as she was packing up and moving out. Both of us were screaming nasty things at each other from across the parking lot. We could have been the Real Housewives of the Bay Area with the way we were acting. How embarrassing, and how ridiculous we must have looked.

We barely talked for a couple of years. The friendship appeared to be lost.

Gina's son later started attending pre-school at Berkeley Youth Alternatives. Gina and Taruk ran into each other and had a good conversation in his office. I saw her another time at BYA and she complimented me on how thin I looked and how happy I seemed.

It was nice for us to catch up, but not quite enough to fix some of the damage that had been done in our friendship. It was a couple of years later, after Taruk's disappearance, that we ran into each other again at a restaurant and had a nice, long talk. Eventually, the wounds healed and we reunited as best buds.

I couldn't have been more grateful to have her friendship back because I desperately needed it on that day, in December 2008.

I drove over to her place and we just cried. I don't know what I would have done without her. You need friends to lean on at times like that and she came through for me. She's a very sensitive person. She tried to keep me sane, which wasn't easy.

"You'll be all right," she said. "At least you know now."

I told her about Taruk's mom saying that she wished Hasira hadn't told police about Taruk's body. Gina couldn't believe it, either. When I talked to Sue again, I had the call on speaker phone so Gina could listen in.

Sue started going on and on about all of the television crews in the parking lot at the apartments. She was laughing about it. Then she started talking about Taruk and said, "You were smart not to divorce that bastard 'cause you're going to get everything."

That's what she was thinking about? Her son was dead, buried right below her, but her mind was on ownership of the apartments and money. It reminded me of Hassan's obsession with the building.

It made me start thinking more about Hassan's motives in killing Taruk and burying him the way he did.

Gina could see me starting to boil, so she took the phone out of my hand and hung up on her. I was furious with Sue. So was Gina. We pulled into the parking lot at Chevys, a Mexican restaurant not far from where Gina lived, went inside and took a seat at the bar.

I couldn't get myself together. I would be talking, and the next moment, I'd burst out in tears again. The tears just kept coming in waves. I couldn't stop them.

I wanted a drink, but couldn't collect my thoughts long enough to place the order. The bartender came over, asked what was wrong and insisted that she had just the drink for us.

The ingredients were rum, peach Schnapps, Triple Sec, Grenadine and pineapple juice. It was a real deep blue color. I took a sip and asked her what the drink was called. She answered, "It's called a 'Superman.'"

I immediately broke down again. How ironic, huh? I had often said that Taruk's problems were partly because he felt so invincible, "like he was Superman."

Now, we were mourning his bizarre death with a drink they called "Superman." It was one more oddity in this insane story that had taken over my life.

We only had one or two of the drinks. It tasted great, but was ridiculously strong, sort of like a Long Island Iced Tea. Both of us were drunk.

I just sat there in shock, wondering how and why this all could have happened with Taruk, going back almost five years to when his drug relapse started.

One day, we're living a great life, everything seemed perfect, then he reverted to his dark side for about five months before suddenly disappearing.

What kept going through my mind was all the pain I had endured when he supposedly left me. My ego was shattered. Whether I wanted to admit it or not, my mindset would be different from that day forward. Thinking that Taruk had left me, with no explanation, had permanently changed me, and not in a good way.

I often thought about how, when you end a relationship, you typically have the opportunity and freedom to call, text and e-mail that person directly to tell them what a jerk they are. You get the opportunity to re-hash all the crap that you had put each other through.

You can get that out of your system. It helps you to move on. But I didn't have that chance to vent.

I didn't know what happened or why. It honestly would have been easier to catch him in bed with another woman. Then I would have a reason to loathe him. Instead, I was in this weird state of limbo.

And now, 4 1/2 years later, the mourning was starting up for the second time. Round 2, just as fresh as the first time.

Nothing creates a string of memories quite like a death. Gina and I shared stories in our drunken state. It was therapeutic for both of us.

She talked about the first time she saw Taruk. He had come to the office to pick me up. Gina was working at the front desk and saw him walk in. She grabbed the phone, kneeled down and called me. "He is so fine," she said, as we both broke into laughter. New relationships are so exciting. We were like school girls. She was so happy for me.

That's Gina. She's very personable and fun. She's a good mother and a hard worker. She went back to school when she was in her 30's to pursue a career as an ultrasound physician assistant or radiologist.

Gina said that she thought Taruk had a great influence on my son. Jordan, like many young kids, was overly active. He would climb under tables and make you chase him down in stores. He did it to me and to Gina.

It had gotten so ridiculous that I stopped chasing him. We made a deal where he would tell me what part of the store he was going to be in, and promise not to leave. When I got in line to check out, I would ask the clerk to get on the loud speaker and call Jordan up to the front of the store so we could leave. It took the stress out of shopping. One time, the knucklehead turned it around on me, though. He went to the clerk and had them call my name.

Another time, when Jordan was a little older, he started looking around for Taruk and I in the store. But we had both gone to use the restrooms. Jordan couldn't find us anywhere, so he went out to the parking lot to search.

We came out of the bathrooms and started looking around for him, thinking that he had vanished. I was in a panic, absolutely starting to freak out. A woman saw me and pointed outside. Jordan was standing next to the car.

She told me, "You looked scared and that look always pertains to children. You both (Jordan and I) look exactly alike."

Jordan is independent and those might have been signs that he was starting to try to pull away from his mom at a young age. He needed some discipline, especially from a male. Gina said that she thought Taruk had helped to calm Jordan down and get him under control.

Jordan turned 18 in the summer of 2011. He's become a very laid-back guy, a man of very few words. He's loyal, loving, generous and funny. My baby is now 6' 1", 210 pounds, with a handsome warm smile, green eyes and brown hair. I do think that Taruk had a good influence on him, despite it all.

Gina had a good chuckle, too, when she recalled how Taruk had been nice enough to return a hair dryer she left behind when she moved, but that he had kept a rug of hers because it was black and silver, Raiders colors.

We laughed. We cried. We laughed. We cried. And then we cried some more.

The wounds were all reopening for me. I desperately missed Taruk all over again, even more than during the first mourning, because this time, I knew he hadn't just dumped me. I was mad because the special times we had together had been stolen from us.

I missed lying in bed with him while the both of us read. In early 2003, Taruk and I decided to get rid of the television in our room and read every night instead. I was an avid reader and he started to become one, too. I would read the book first, then he would read it, and then we'd discuss it. We had our own husband-and-wife book club going.

I kept thinking about Taruk's sense of humor, too. He could always make me laugh, even on my worst day. Jordan is a slow, lazy walker at times, and

Taruk would tell him, "This isn't a nursing home, let's go."

Meanwhile, Jordan's friend, Steven, was tall and chunky, while Jordan was a skinny kid. Taruk and I were waiting to pick them up at the movies one afternoon. They were late, and when they finally showed up, Taruk said, "Hey look, it's Fatman and Robin." The nickname stuck. From then on, Steven and Jordan were Fatman and Robin, the dynamic duo.

It was always good-natured teasing and made Taruk a lot of fun to be around. It just crushed me now to stop and think about how he must have died. I had no doubt that his father somehow killed him and hid him in that wall. So much for resting in peace.

Watching and reading the news reports over the next few days and weeks was heart-wrenching. It was front-page news for a while in the Bay Area.

The Oakland Tribune reported that police had obtained the search warrant for the building on Wednesday, December 17. They broke down a temporary wall and found the hidden wooden coffin on the first floor, where there is a common area, at least one apartment and a laundry room used by tenants.

The newspaper report added, "Wearing white hazardous-material suits and oxygen masks, crews went into the first floor of the eight-unit complex with shovels and hauled out red trash bags full of unknown materials and huge pieces of wood, including a 6-foot-long box that looked like a homemade coffin."

Although neighbors never called police to report a foul smell, sources said that the stench was overwhelming once the wall came down, the Tribune reported.

Law enforcement sources told the San Francisco Chronicle, "The body had been wrapped in a tarp inside the coffin" and that "the area where the coffin was found was filled with dirt and lime, and someone had left air fresheners there to mask the smell."

Investigator Phillips Abrams of the Berkeley Police Department (BPD) described the scene in an official police report. Acting on the tip from Hasira, the BPD began an "investigative dig in the laundry-room area," Abrams wrote.

"While digging, a wood makeshift coffin in a homemade crypt was found," Abrams added. "The BPD was able to determine that there were human bones inside the coffin. All police activity stopped and the Coroner's Bureau was notified of the find."

The report went on to say that police had talked to Sue Johnson, who told them that, about four years earlier, Hassan had called Tina, the mother of Taruk's daughter, and said, "Taruk has gotten involved with some bad people. He won't be contacting you anymore, but don't worry, I will continue to send you your child support."

After interviewing Tina, the Oakland Tribune confirmed that during Taruk's disappearance, child-support payments for their daughter always arrived from Hassan.

The San Francisco Chronicle interviewed Tom Lindstrom, 61 at the time, who was living in an apartment on the first floor. Lindstrom said that Hassan had removed locker space from the laundry room from as far back as 1995, in order to convert the area into a livable space. "It was a little bit of a bunker," Lindstrom said.

Lindstrom called Hassan "the most self-serving guy I've ever met in my life." He also told the newspaper that Hassan "enjoyed being an academician" and projected an image of being well-schooled even though he had "no degrees."

According to the Chronicle article, "Lindstrom, who is a quadriplegic, said he broke his leg in August (2008) and hired an 18-year-old woman to be his live-in attendant. He was dissatisfied with her, however, and tried to fire her while he was in the hospital.

"(Hassan Ben-Ali), however, persuaded him to allow the woman to stay on. Lindstrom said he later found out that an acquaintance of the woman's had also moved into (Lindstrom's) apartment while he was recovering in a hospital and nursing home."

Lindstrom told the Chronicle: "They had turned my place upside down. The way (Hassan) took advantage of me living here was insane."

The scuttlebutt concerning a motive for Hassan's suicide became intriguing. Slowly but surely, the pieces started to come together. A day after Taruk's body was discovered, the Oakland Tribune reported that Hassan may have hidden the body "in order to continue collecting rent and running the rental property."

"Sources also said another person - unknown to police at this time - may have known about the secret burial and was extorting money from Hassan (Ben-Ali) to keep quiet about the situation," the Tribune reported on December 19.

Neighbors also told the Tribune that Hassan had acted "paranoid and scared" before his death. Hassan also apparently had admitted to someone that the Internal Revenue Service was after him.

All of this information started leaking out only after Hasira wrote a letter and shared her story with police. I have to give her credit. If she didn't come forward, we might never have known the truth about what had happened to Taruk, along with many of the other details that would come out in time.

Hasira is a white woman who always dressed in Muslim garb. I only saw her one time in street clothes. That was for a dinner party at our house. She was nice, but odd.

In her letter, which was given to police, Hasira discussed her relationship with Hassan. "I became intimately involved with Hassan subsequent to a 'vision' we both had, simultaneously, wherein I was 'handed over' to him," she wrote. "I have always believed this to be a vision from The Creator, thus I have always called myself married to Hassan."

She added, "My four children have never accepted that event as either a vision from God or a marriage, believing it to be the workings of Hassan's and/or his mother's witchcraft."

Hasira went on to suggest that Hassan's mother was a witch and had used voodoo on her. "I could feel the needles she was using on a doll," wrote Hasira, who also indicated that Hassan and Taruk might have had special powers.

With all I knew about her background, I didn't consider her tip to be anywhere close to credible. I figured that she probably just had another of her so-called visions.

But apparently, Hassan had really confided in her. She was being honest, although her version was strictly based on what Hassan had told her.

One part that I certainly disputed was the notion that Taruk, like Hassan, had committed suicide. According to Hasira's letter, Taruk "could not live a double life anymore, i.e., being a drug addict and a gang member while showing a face to the world of a good citizen, i.e., a (counselor), husband, and father to his daughter and step-son - all of which he did a great job at!"

Hasira said that she first met Taruk, who was 18 at the time, in September 1986. She said that she negotiated a rental agreement with Taruk because her "new landlord," Hassan, was vacationing in Hawaii. Hassan still owned the Ashby apartments at that point. It was one of about 27 properties that he owned at various times.

Hasira wrote that Hassan told her, "Taruk's overdosing on heroin was a suicide because Taruk had said a bunch of 'goodbyes' to a lot of people to whom he was close."

I talked to as many of Taruk's friends as I could after he disappeared, and no one said anything like that to me. They hadn't seen or heard from Taruk, either.

"My position," Hasira wrote, "is that it is not a coincidence that there are two suicides in this family for the very same reason - inability to live a double life. The witches made their charges commit suicide."

Besides Hasira's letter, more details on Hassan's suicide started to come out when a copy of a holographic will for him was discovered. It was basically in the form of a suicide letter.

The will was dated Nov. 3, 2008, and directed to Ian Rolde, Hassan's lawyer. The translation of the difficult-to-decipher handwritten letter reads as follows:

*Dear (Ian); Unfortunately your reading of this means I had to exit or was exited.*

*The story begins in June of 2004. Taruk, as you know had a lengthy record of drug abuse. On 6 June 04 he registered at the motel (near?) Kaiser Oakland. We spoke several times in person and on the phone. What came to make sense later were his words asking me to tell his child's mother-the child he loved them.*

*I responded at the time why don't you do it yourself. Dumb assed me. Around 3 p.m. or so I tried to reach him*

*on the phone & could not get thru. So, I drove over &*
*found him clearly having removed himself from this life.*
*Perhaps there was nothing I or anyone could have done*
*to avert this but, who knows. I totally freaked out - back*
*Taruk - Taruk was a very proud man and never wished*
*for anyone to see him in a weakened state - & God forbid*
*- that it should be public about his drug addiction.*

*I respect his wishes & I & Waldo Rodriguez*
*(Murphy) moved him into a vehicle and ferried him*
*away. Regardless of Taruk's (his) wishes, I should have*
*notified the authorities. Big mistake.*

*Waldo - 21 yrs of age at the time of this writing at*
*some point decided to go into the extortion business &*
*coerced me via threats to give him a great sum of $ just*
*how much I don't know. The (receptions?) (Bank) are*
*available and will be more accessible to you. He and his*
*lover Klara are a team in this dark enterprise. The vari-*
*ety of threats includes the police & his woman's Miami*
*family - who would seize me & in some way take over the*
*Bldg. None of these outcomes is appealing.*

*There is a will (Taruk's) leaving the bldg. to me -*
*but at this point what would I (dead) have for it. So I*
*would like to appoint (Sue) Ben-Ali, his mom as my ben-*
*eficiary. I hope this rather over simple will, will do. &*
*please - do not let this asshole get away with his black*
*deeds. He has ruined me & pushed me into taking my*
*life or worse (abduction) He is a sociopath and capable of*
*anything.*

*– Hassan Ben-Ali.*

Hassan's story certainly appeared to have the
dates twisted. He made a reference to Taruk being

at the hotel on June 6. He then made it sound as if he had found Taruk dead that same day.

However, I had talked to Taruk on the phone on June 8, the day he actually went missing.

The holographic will, supposedly written by Hassan several weeks before his suicide, left everything to his ex-wife. But Hassan didn't write "Sue Johnson", he wrote Sue "Ben-Ali." Sue had been divorced from Hassan for more than two decades. She'd been married to Brad Johnson for 15 years.

Sue Ben-Ali? How bizarre is that?

And now, unbelievably, we had to ask the age-old question, "Where's Waldo?"

Waldo Rodriguez, who apparently has many aliases, was a Cuban kid from Florida who was one of Hassan's young "pet projects." He had lived with Taruk, Jordan and me for a while. Jordan didn't like him at all, but I didn't know whether Waldo really could have been involved in hiding Taruk's body and blackmailing Hassan. It seemed too farfetched.

But the story was taking on a life of its own, so who knew? The "facts" were all coming through Hassan in some form, whether in his will/suicide letter or from what he had told Hasira. You never knew what Hassan might fabricate to try to protect himself and his reputation or to take down someone else.

Police didn't contact me until several days after Taruk's body was discovered. I found out that Sue had already told them that Taruk had died of a drug overdose. I couldn't figure out how she had come to that conclusion. She couldn't have known that for a fact.

She also didn't inform police that Taruk had a wife. Tina, the mother of Taruk's daughter, was the one who actually told police I existed.

It was probably a blessing. The media would have been all over me and Jordan. By the time the police contacted me, things had settled down and most of the media had moved on to the next gruesome headline.

Authorities still needed someone to officially identify Taruk's body. I was able to do that because I knew he had a horrific scar on his left ankle from a car accident.

I dreaded having to be the one to identify him, but it wasn't that bad. We actually did it all over the phone. I couldn't take seeing him in person. They asked about any marks or scars. I told them that he had skin grafts taken from his thigh and placed on his ankle. There was a horrible scar and a metal pin in the ankle, which I'm sure made for an easier confirmation.

He also had two tattoos on his chest - a "mad Arab" and "SF" for San Francisco 49ers. They could see the scar on his ankle and remnants of the "SF" to confirm that it was him.

I continued to wait for the results from the coroner's report. I was getting anxious to know as many of the facts as possible. What would it say, if anything, about Taruk's death?

I didn't believe that it was suicide by drug overdose, because I had talked to Taruk earlier in the day when he went missing. He was not high and did not sound like someone who was going to get high in the next few hours. That didn't make sense to me, despite his documented drug problems.

When the report came back, it read: "Cause of death not determined by autopsy or toxicology (advanced decomposition)."

On April 23, 2009, the Oakland Tribune reported that Mike Yost, Alameda County's supervising coroner investigator, said toxicology tests on the tissues and skin of Taruk's remains were "negative for everything."

The headline read: "Toxicology Tests On Man Found Entombed in Berkeley Basement Don't Show Drug Overdose."

The Tribune story quoted Yost, saying, "Of course, it was a long time (that the body was there) and odds of anything being found were slim."

Officer Andrew Frankel, a police spokesman, told the Oakland Tribune that police had a working theory that Hassan killed himself "because of guilt over his son and the possibility that someone was blackmailing him because of the secret burial."

The police didn't know how to even prosecute such a case. Was Taruk murdered? Was it suicide? Accidental drug overdose? At the very least, Hassan was guilty of the improper burial of human remains, but I suspected, and still suspect, that it was much more, that he was also responsible for Taruk's death.

"Even if (Hassan Ben-Ali) was being blackmailed, (he and his son) are gone, so there's no way to know," Frankel told the Oakland Tribune.

Frankel added, "I've never seen a case unravel quite like this in my eight years in the department."

Waldo was nowhere to be found. There were rumors that he had gone back to Florida.

Hasira certainly seemed adamant that Hassan was being blackmailed by someone.

"Hassan did not tell me he was being black-mailed until one month before he took his life," she wrote in her letter. "And, he did not tell me of Taruk's death or the whereabouts of his body until less than one week before he took his own life - just in case anyone was wondering what my role was in all of this."

Hasira ended the letter, saying, "I hope that this divulging of my experience of this fiasco helps the police find and punish the real criminals!"

One of those criminals, Hassan Ben-Ali, had already punished himself. With his death came many questions that needed to be answered.

# CHAPTER 7

Losing Taruk the second time hurt in a different way.

Before, I felt like the victim. This time, he was the victim. I hurt for him and I had to try to find out the truth. I owed it to Taruk. I also had to do it for my own peace of mind.

There was an intense curiosity growing inside of me. I smelled a rat. I knew where he had lived. I knew what he had looked like. I knew how he had acted. I just had to figure out how he did it.

For 4 1/2 years, I had been wondering how that apartment building possibly kept running in Taruk's absence. I got my chance to start searching for answers after being appointed as the special administrator for Taruk's estate in February 2009, two months after his body was discovered.

I had been taking some on-line classes with Novus Law School. My interest in the law and in solving murders and crimes went back many years. I was always drawn to those types of books.

But it didn't take a criminal-justice major or investigative reporter to identify the scam that Hassan had been running. It just took a little digging.

A trip to the Berkeley Housing Authority was the turning point. I introduced myself and explained that I was in charge of the apartment building in the wake of Taruk's death, and I needed to obtain some information from them. The woman told me that she had dealt with my husband, Taruk, and offered her condolences.

I immediately thought something was odd, because it sounded as if she had seen him recently. At least, that's what I suspected. Out of curiosity, I asked her to describe Taruk. The person she described was a dark-skinned, older man. Taruk, of course, was light skinned and younger.

I told her, "That wasn't my husband. That was his father, Hassan, who hid Taruk in a wall, and then committed suicide."

She had seen the story in the newspapers and on TV, just like almost everyone else in the Bay Area. She was stunned. Her mouth dropped.

Several of the other employees at the Housing Authority also confirmed that Hassan had been going there and impersonating Taruk for years.

That was a big piece to the puzzle, and some of the other pieces then fell into place easily. As they say, follow the money. It was all there in black and white, and easy to trace.

Everywhere that Taruk did business for the building, Hassan showed up. He was no longer Hassan; he had become Taruk, his son.

The only exception was the tax guy, Jeffrey Lee, who knew Taruk personally. I had introduced them. So Hassan went in there "on Taruk's behalf."

Hassan got away with this masquerade for more than four years, and even opened up credit cards and wrote checks on Taruk's bank account. No one, of course, knew that Taruk was dead.

The trail of checks was alarming. I couldn't believe that he had pulled this off for so long. You wonder how long he could have kept it up if he hadn't taken his own life.

The checks to "Waldo Murphy" totaled around $200,000 over four years. During a six-day period in late June 2008, there were four checks to Waldo for $4,000 each time. Then on August 1, the amount was $20,000.

It was all extortion, black-mail money to keep Waldo quiet after he helped Hassan hide Taruk's body.

Hassan created his own little signature on the checks. He wasn't actually signing Taruk's name. He just made sort of a circle. That's how he signed all the checks.

I looked back at the wedding certificate for Taruk and I. Hassan had signed that as a witness. It was nothing like how he had signed the checks on Taruk's account.

Hassan had traveled all over the world on his missing son's money. He led people to believe that he was this eccentric property owner, while hiding all his deep, dark secrets. Hasira, his long-time girl-friend, wife, whatever you want to call her, didn't even know the truth. She thought that Hassan owned the building all along. She never knew Taruk was the true owner.

While going through all the bank documents, I also found a check written for $50,000 on June 29, 2008.

It was made out to Farrah, the wife of JJ, a friend of Taruk's. Hassan used to call JJ his son and Taruk called him a brother. JJ lived with them during some of those wild times when Taruk was younger, but he had grown up, settled down and became a real-estate agent.

The 50 grand apparently was payment for JJ's role in helping to push through a loan when Hassan refinanced the apartment building. JJ was the loan officer. I just wondered why the check was written to his wife and not to him.

I liked JJ. He seemed normal, was well-spoken and fun to be around. His dad was from somewhere in Europe. His mom had been friends with Hassan. He had a very unusual first name, I couldn't pronounce it nor could I spell it. I believe it was made up by JJ. I'm not sure if he had it legally changed or not. Everybody just knew him as JJ.

He attended the memorial service that we held for Taruk. JJ was hurting. He started crying. He said, "Hassan told me that Taruk was in Mexico and that he had OK'd all this stuff (for the loan). So I pushed it through."

JJ was living with his wife in the Ashby apartments while Taruk was still alive, before moving sometime in 2004. I really believe that he didn't know about the scam Hassan was running. I think he trusted Hassan because they went back so many years, and ended up getting used by Hassan.

Nevertheless, JJ soon disappeared after the funeral, presumably so he wouldn't have to repay the money. I have no idea where he and Farrah went.

Wells Fargo was angry, not surprisingly, but the bank eventually did reverse the refinancing loan and returned the estate back to where it was in 2004 when Taruk went missing, a difference of about $150,000.

Another bank, however, still owes the estate $250,000 for all of the fraudulent checks that Hassan wrote, which did not support the running of the building during the time.

I also got a letter from 9 Dragons, a company where Hassan had forged Taruk's name to receive another loan. After my attorney contacted them with proof of the forgery, they dropped their lien for $100,000 against the estate.

The estate is worth around $1.5 million with the apartment building as the primary asset.

Hassan's deception became a classic example around the country for fraud. Fidelity National Financial - a leading provider of title insurance, specialty insurance and claims management ser-vices - wrote about Hassan under the heading "Most Bizarre Claim Ever?" in its "FraudInsights" newsletter dated July 2010.

The report reads as follows:

*Title insurance policies insure 100 percent against forgery. If the insured party can prove documents in the transaction were forged, they are entitled to reimbursement of their losses. The problem is how to prove a forgery. In this case, the lender had the documented support of a police investigation.*

*Liberty Title, a title agent for Lawyers Title Insurance Company, issued a loan policy on June 20, 2008 for $600,000 to JP Morgan Chase. Later, JP Morgan Chase was served with a Summons and Complaint: a Special Administrator had been appointed to the case (by the State of California) due to the suicide of the borrower who had no heirs to his estate. The Special Administrator filed a complaint with the courts to void the $600,000 mortgage, citing forgery.*

*The State of California determined the loan was a forgery based on a police investigation, which showed that on December 15, 2008, Hassan Ben-Ali committed suicide by shooting himself in the head. While the police were at the scene, the purported wife of Ben-Ali advised police that Ben-Ali was feeling guilty because four years ago (2004), Ben-Ali's son, Taruk, apparently overdosed and died in an Oakland motel room. Hassan retrieved his son's body, and took it back to the apartment building that was vested in his son's name. Ben-Ali wrapped his son's body in a clear plastic bag, then a blanket, then two tarps and placed it in a crypt. Ben-Ali then filled the crypt with dirt and sealed it by cementing a block wall around it in the apartment building's laundry room. Ben-Ali then assumed his son's identity, and on June 20, 2008 obtained a $600,000 mortgage against the apartment building. The proceeds of the loan were used to pay off an existing loan in the amount of $464,065.96 and the balance of the funds was given to Ben-Ali. Ben-Ali made* *the payments until he committed suicide and default occurred.*

*The Claims department agreed to permit JP Morgan Chase to enter into a settlement agreement with the Special Administrator while the claim was being processed. The settlement was to forfeit any claim over and above the $464,065.96 equitable subrogation figure.*

*In a nutshell, equitable subrogation occurs when the proceeds from one mortgagee's loan are utilized to satisfy the outstanding obligations under an earlier mortgage. Equitable subrogation affords the second mortgagee the right to be substituted into the position of the earlier mortgagee and afford priority over subsequent liens and creditors - to the extent the loan satisfied the earlier debt. As a result, this claim cost the Company $135,934.04 (the difference between the prior mortgage and the new mortgage) - not the full amount of the new mortgage, which was $600,000.*

*While extremely bizarre, this claim provides our readers an inside look at how claims are negotiated to make the insured party whole without overcharging the Company.*

When Hassan pulled off the refinancing hoax, Waldo received a lot of that money. He also gave Waldo cars, including a Ford SUV and probably Taruk's missing BMW.

I was able to help uncover the fraud by poring through all the records, and I let everybody know exactly what Hassan had been doing. I think some other people around him would have been just fine covering it all up.

The police, meanwhile, found what was purportedly Taruk's will in the bunker of the apartment, near the location where his body was discovered.

I never met the Sergeant who was handling the case, but we talked several times over the phone. He called and asked if I had ever signed a will for Taruk. I told him that I had not.

He said, "I have an invalid will here because (Ian Rolde, Hassan's lawyer) signed a will."

I said, "I don't know anything about it."

"This will's invalid," the Sergeant repeated. "(Ian Rolde) signed it and he's a beneficiary in the will. This is definitely invalid."

I first saw a copy of this obviously fake will on February 5, 2009. Sue Johnson, Taruk's mother, e-mailed it to me.

One of the "witnesses" was signed "Wendy Ben-Ali." It was forged. The Wendy part of the signature actually looked like my writing, but I never signed a will for Taruk.

The date on the document was August 16, 2002, two weeks after we were married. Taruk and I had left early in the morning on the 17th, for our honeymoon in Hawaii. He had never said anything about having a will or doing any estate planning.

I reiterated to the Sergeant that I had never heard or seen anything about this alleged will before, but I kept wondering how the Wendy part of the signature could look so real.

I talked to my mom about it and she reminded me of the document that Hassan had me sign in 2004. It was when he tried to get me to sign the divorce papers after Taruk disappeared. I wouldn't sign those, but he also asked me to sign a piece of paper that supposedly would allow Taruk to receive immediate medical attention if needed.

I believe that Waldo was there, too, and we were sitting out on my patio. I signed something. But did I sign "Wendy *Ben-Ali*"? That's still perplexing to me, because I did not use Taruk's last name. I signed everything "Wendy *Wilburn.*" The only other exception I can remember was for the timeshare in Vegas. I know I signed "Ben-Ali" for that.

Could I have also signed "Ben-Ali" for the medical paper? It's possible, I guess. Maybe I did it just to make sure there would be no questions if Taruk needed treatment. I really don't remember. I was upset that Hassan had come over, asking me to divorce Taruk in the first place.

But I know that I didn't sign a will for Taruk. Not in 2002, not in 2004, not ever. I would have told him to find another witness, if not another wife, based on what was written in this will.

I had only signed that one piece of paper. The contents had to do with giving Taruk medical help if he was dying. I do remember it was very simplistic. One sheet and that was it.

Was that signature then somehow transferred to the fake will? Did someone copy my signature and then forge the will?

Perhaps the only two people who know the truth are Hassan and Waldo. One is dead, the other one can't be found.

Or maybe there's one other person who knows, someone who could undeservingly benefit. I wonder who that could be.

In my opinion, the fake will was written in the third person by Hassan. It appointed Hassan as the executor. The surprising alternate executor was Ian Rolde, Hassan's lawyer. His last name had been spelled incorrectly, leaving off the "e."

The will referred to me not by name, but as the "wife," and left me with Taruk's personal property. That would have included his 2002 BMW, a Rolex watch and some antique furniture that he had over at Hassan's apartment, except everything was gone.

The timing of this agreement, two weeks after getting married, was another clue that it couldn't have been legitimate. You're a newlywed, about to go on your honeymoon, and you sign a will that leaves nothing for your wife in the event of your death? It just doesn't make any sense.

The will also claimed to leave Taruk's daughter, Tiffany, a $250,000 insurance policy on his life, which was to be held in trust with Hassan. However, the policy no longer existed because payments hadn't been made in years. The fake will also listed an incorrect date of birth for Tiffany.

Another $250,000 insurance policy that had previously existed with me as the beneficiary was also null and void because payments had stopped.

The only insurance policy that was still active listed Hassan as the beneficiary. It was with Hartford Insurance, an accidental death policy for the same amount: $250,000.

Back in 2002, Taruk had showed me the two polices with Tiffany and myself as the beneficiaries.

The one for me was new at the time. Tiffany's had already existed.

I went through all the bank records and confirmed that there had been no payments on either policy in years. The only insurance policy that continued to be paid was the one with Hassan as the beneficiary. Those $84 monthly payments had been paid religiously up until his death.

Hassan, obviously, couldn't stand me, so he wasn't going to pay on a life insurance policy that listed me as the beneficiary. No surprise there. But stopping payments on the one for his granddaughter showed his true side.

Titled "LAST WILL AND TESTAMENT OF TARUK JOSEPH BEN-ALI," the fake will reads as follows:

*I, TARUK JOSEPH BEN-ALI, of Berkeley, County of Alameda, State of California, being over the age of legal majority and of sound and disposing mind and memory, and not acting under duress, menace, fraud or the undue influence of any person whomsoever, do herby make, publish, and declare this to be my Last Will and Testament in the manner following, and I say:*

*FIRST: I hereby revoke any and all Wills and Codicils to Wills heretofore made by me.*

*SECOND: I hereby declare that I am married. I have one living child, (Tiffany), born 7/31/93. I have no other children and no descendants of any deceased children.*

*THIRD: I hereby give, devise and bequeath all of my personal property to my wife, to be disposed of as she see fits.*

FOURTH: I hereby direct my Executor, hereinafter named, to pay all of my just debts; expenses of last illness and funeral, as soon after my death as can be done legally and conveniently. Upon my death my assets shall be sold or value transferred at the discretion of the Executor, and the proceeds shall be distributed as follows: to my father, Hassan Ben-Ali. My daughter (Tiffany) has been provided for by a life insurance policy on my life, which is held in trust for her by my father, Hassan Ben-Ali.

FIFTH: I have intentionally omitted to provide anything for any and all of my heirs who have not been specifically herein mentioned. If any devisee, legatee or beneficiary under this Will, or any other person claiming under or through any devisee, legatee or beneficiary, or any other person who would be entitled to share in my estate through intestate succession, shall in any manner whatsoever, directly or indirectly, contest this Will or attack, oppose or in any manner seek to impair or invalidate any provision thereof, or shall in any manner whatsoever conspire to cooperate with any person or persons attempting to do any of the acts or things aforesaid, or shall acquiesce in or fail to oppose such proceedings, then in each of the abovementioned cases I hereby bequeath to such person or persons the sum of ONE DOLLAR ($1.00) only, and all other bequests, devises and interests in this Will given to such person or persons shall be forfeited and shall be distributed pro rata among such of my devisees, legatees, and beneficiaries as shall not in any manner have participated in, and as shall have opposed, such acts or proceedings.

SIXTH: I hereby nominate and appoint Hassan Ben-Ali as the Executor of this my Last Will and Testament, *to act as such without bond in any of the proceedings in the administration of my estate.*

*I hereby empower my said Executor to do and perform any and all acts necessary in the matter of the conduct of my estate without an order of the Court therefore, and in the event of the sale of any of the property of my estate I hereby authorize and direct my said Executor to make the same at public or private sale, with or without notice, as my said Executor may determine, subject only to confirmation by the Court.*

*In the event my above named Executor shall be unable to or refused to act as such, then and in that event, I hereby nominate and appoint Attorney (Ian Rolde) of Oakland, California as my alternate Executor, to serve as such without bond, with all the powers heretofore conferred by this Paragraph.*

*SEVENTH: In the event that both the above-named persons shall be unable or refuse to act as Executor, the Court shall then nominate and appoint a person to serve as such Administrator in any of the proceedings in the administration of my estate.*

*IN WITNESS WHEREOF, I have hereunto set my hand at Oakland, California this August 16, 2002 in the presence of witnesses requested by me to act as such.*

It was then signed by Taruk Ben-Ali. There were two witness signatures. One was the forged "Wendy Ben-Ali." The other was illegible. No one could figure out what it said. The Police Sergeant had told me that Ian signed the will. He must have thought the second witness was Ian. More than likely, it was Hassan's scribbling.

The nature of the will is truly comical on many levels to me, but none more so than the idea of Taruk naming Ian Rolde as the alternate executor. That's absolutely slapstick. Taruk was more likely to leave his estate to his barber than to Ian Rolde.

Hassan had asked Ian, a prominent lawyer in the Bay Area, to represent Taruk when Taruk got in trouble with the law.

But Taruk didn't really like him. Ian was short, shifty and always looked frazzled. Taruk called him "seedy." Ian always wanted something for nothing.

Ian didn't respond to calls from the police at first, until it came out that he was mentioned in Taruk's will. Then he made himself available.

Sometime in late January to early February, Ian contacted me about splitting the estate in an out-of-court agreement. He was trying to assure himself of some money. He said that we could avoid the probate lawyers and all those hassles. By making an agreement amongst ourselves, it never would have to go to court.

I asked him, "Why are you even involved?"

His response: "Because I was the lawyer and Hassan told me, a long time ago, that I deserve some of the building."

I didn't know whether to laugh or scream.

"What does something Hassan told you have to do with Taruk's estate?" I asked.

The conversation took place over the phone. I explained to Ian that I simply couldn't understand why he should get a percentage of the building.

"You're a lawyer; you're a friend. Why would you get a percentage of a family-owned building?" I said. "You get paid for being a lawyer."

He repeated himself, saying that the promise had been made years ago. Ian then laid out a plan in which Sue Johnson and I would each get 40 percent while Ian took 20 percent. He apparently didn't know about Tiffany, Taruk's daughter, at the time.

After I immediately rejected the ridiculous offer, Ian moved on and tried to negotiate with Tiffany's mother, Tina.

Tina is a nice-looking black woman whose heart always seemed to be in the right place. She cares about her daughter and was trying to do the best thing possible for Tiffany. Ian suggested breaking it up four ways, 25 percent to him, Tiffany, Sue and me.

Ian asked us all to consider his proposals. I didn't consider them for a second. He had no business getting a penny.

Hassan had made a verbal promise on something that Hassan didn't even own. Ian knew that. He was just hoping we'd cave and give him a piece of the pie.

I would have rather thrown the pie in his face. There was no way I was going to agree to give Ian a cut, just so we could avoid going to probate court.

Ian wasn't the only one who moved in and tried to position himself for a share of something he didn't deserve. So did Art Floyd.

I had never even heard of Floyd before 2007. Jordan and Tiffany had become friends and were spending some time together. Jordan ended up meeting Art through Tiffany. Jordan said that he was "a tall, nice guy."

That's all I knew about Art at that time. As it turned out, Hassan was his father. As far as I know, and I'm 99.9 percent certain of this, Taruk never even knew that he had a half-brother.

Art's mother was a white woman from San Francisco. Art was living right there in the Bay Area. I guess after he and Hassan found each other, they started spending time together. They went on bicycle rides, which was one of Hassan's hobbies.

Art doesn't say much, but I believe he's a nice guy. He just got caught up in this ugly web of deceit. I received a phone call from him just days after Hassan's suicide and Taruk's body was found.

He introduced himself as the son of Hassan, and Taruk's brother. At one point in the conversation, he mentioned that police had told him they'd found Taruk's purported will.

The first time I actually met Art was at a memorial service for Taruk. We didn't get off to a great start. Hassan apparently had told him that Taruk and I were divorced. Art was fighting me and trying to inherit part of Taruk's estate.

I told him at one point, "Who are you? I don't even know you."

Art, along with Tina, was involved in getting me removed as the special administrator. I was in charge of the estate for about 3-4 months. Art and Tina didn't think I should have that kind of control.

The court then appointed Duane Leonard to be the special administrator. He was a capable older gentleman who quickly became friends with Sue. She basically took over as resident manager for the apartments.

Sue had given Art the keys to Hassan's apartment so he could remove some of his dad's stuff. He also kept some mail for both Hassan and the building, and even some of Taruk's belongings.

Because Art also didn't return the keys for Hassan's apartment, we were unable to re-rent the two-bedroom unit for a couple months, which resulted in a loss of income for the estate.

While he released some of the mail to Sue Johnson, there were bills that weren't forwarded to us. I think it was the water company that told me that the mail was being returned to them every time.

Plain and simple, Art wasn't forthright in helping Sue and I administer the building. Why he did that, I don't know. I believe that he was destroyed by the news of his dad's suicide. His father had told him so many lies. He was dealing with the fact that he didn't really know his dad and what his dad was capable of.

Art later apologized for making an issue over whether I was truly Taruk's wife. "I was lied to," he said. "I was told that you two had divorced."

Hassan, of course, was the one who had told him the lie. In the end, I felt bad for Art. He was just another victim. He eventually admitted to me that he didn't really deserve any of Taruk's estate.

You have to wonder what kind of relationship the two half-brothers might have had if they'd had the opportunity to meet under normal circumstances.

While all this maneuvering was going on behind the scenes, one thing didn't change. Waldo - a tall, skinny kid who always had a bizarre personality and weird values - still hadn't been found. He was in the Bay Area when the story broke about Hassan's suicide. Waldo left the area immediately.

One of the stories that came out suggested that Waldo had put the "Miami mafia" on Hassan, but that was just another one of Hassan's delusions. Waldo is a jerk, but he wasn't mob-connected. I just think that he got greedier and greedier while threatening to turn Hassan in if Hassan didn't keep giving him more money.

It was a tough case to investigate for the police. Everyone was dead and Waldo was missing. The police Sergeant seemed like a decent man. He got right to the point when we talked. I felt that he was doing the best job he could.

He claimed that he didn't know what really happened, but he did seem to believe there was foul play involved with Taruk's death. The Sergeant also thought Ian was behind the fake will. Those were the only theories he shared with me. I begged for him to continue on the murder path, but he said they needed to find Waldo first. He admitted they might not ever find out exactly what happened.

It appeared to me that they were giving up on the case because of the unusual circumstances. I wasn't all that frustrated by that, but I knew the whole truth had not been told.

To my surprise, I found out in June 2011 that the Berkeley police were still actively searching for Waldo.

In the meantime, Ian, Art, Sue and Tina, who was acting on behalf of her daughter, went ahead with plans to try to settle the estate dispute in court. The first big question would come down to whether Taruk's will was declared valid or invalid.

It had become very annoying, confusing and sad. My interest in continuing in law school and pursuing a career in law was gone. I was very disillusioned by it all.

Even in his death, Hassan was messing with me. I was sure that he was rolling over in his grave, chuckling.

# CHAPTER 8

After all the posturing and back-and-forth discussions about making deals, we prepared to go to court in November 2010 to settle the dispute over who would inherit Taruk's estate, estimated at $1.5 million with the apartment building.

I couldn't believe that I actually had to fight over all of this, especially ownership of the building where Taruk was buried in the wall. That was creepy.

But after living through this nightmare for the last several years, I guess I was getting a little used to creepy.

There were five of us staking claim to the estate in one form or another:

1. Me, Taruk's wife.
2. Tiffany, Taruk's teenage daughter from a previous relationship.
3. Sue Johnson, Taruk's mother.

4. Art Floyd, Taruk's half-brother whom Taruk had never met and apparently didn't even know existed.

5. And Ian Rolde, Hassan's lawyer friend. Rolde was named as the alternate executor (after Hassan) in Taruk's purported will. Ian insisted that he was involved in the court case only out of loyalty to Hassan and Taruk, but I had no doubt that he had cut some type of deal with Sue.

The first - and most crucial - element came down to a judge determining the validity of Taruk's will.

If ruled invalid, Tiffany and I apparently would split the estate 50-50 based on California intestate laws. When a person dies without a legal will in California, the assets are distributed among all living heirs.

The lawyers for Tiffany and I were going to argue vehemently that the will was fake, forged and a total farce.

Sue, Ian and Art wanted to prove just the opposite, that this will for Taruk was real. If ruled valid, Hassan's estate, which was worth next to nothing, would then inherit Taruk's estate.

In Hassan's holographic will, he had left everything to Sue "Ben-Ali" - aka. Sue Johnson - his ex-wife and Taruk's mother. Hassan's will was handwritten by him and dated November 3, 2008, a little over a month before his suicide. Hassan and Sue had been divorced and separated for many years. Sue had remarried.

But Hassan wrote: "I would like to appoint (Sue) Ben-Ali, his (Taruk's) mom as my beneficiary."

So it would be Sue potentially inheriting the entire estate - with nothing going to me, Taruk's wife, or Tiffany, Taruk's daughter.

Ian Rolde was on Sue's side. Based on the wills, Ian had nothing to gain financially. But he still spent a good chunk of money on another attorney to fight that Taruk's will was valid.

It was interesting that Sue had been willing to listen to any and all deals for quite a while, even encouraged them. But she suddenly changed her mind and decided to go for the full estate, minus, of course, whatever she was presumably going to pay Ian to help her.

Sue, by the way, maintained that she hadn't spent a dime on a lawyer. She considered the case Ian's to win or lose.

Art, meanwhile, found himself in an unusual spot. He had been angry with me for not including him in my petition to the court. I felt that he didn't warrant inclusion. He didn't even know Taruk, and my lawyer indicated that Art wasn't owed anything under the circumstances. Under California law, he was not considered an heir to Taruk's estate.

Even if he didn't totally believe that he deserved part of Taruk's will, which he admitted to me, Art was hanging on to some hope that he still might find a way to cash in. He wanted Taruk's will to be ruled valid. If that happened, Art's plan was then to fight Sue Johnson over Hassan's holographic will, which left the entire estate to Sue.

If it came down to Hassan's will, then Art would argue that Hassan had been insane and not capable of writing a will for himself only a few weeks before his suicide.

If Taruk's will was valid and Hassan's will invalid, then Art conceivably could inherit at least part of the estate based on the fact that he's the only living heir of Hassan, other than Tiffany.

In other words, this had gotten so crazy that Art was on the same side as Sue and Ian for Round 1 (over Taruk's will), but would then be pitted against them if there was a potential Round 2 (over Hassan's will).

I just wanted it all to end. Distributing the assets was one more necessary step toward closure.

But it was in the hands of the court system. Not surprisingly, I found out that this was going to take quite a while to complete.

A date would be set for us to go to court, and then it would get changed. This happened over and over, probably 10-15 times.

We had a 60-day delay to allow an opposing counsel time to get its paperwork submitted correctly.

A witness underwent throat surgery, delaying the process for a few months. An attorney had eye surgery, six more weeks.

I went to the court for no reason on several occasions. Other times, my lawyer would appear on my behalf, but I'd have to be on call, within a 20-minute driving distance in case they needed me.

This whole thing started back in January 2009 and we were supposed to go to trial in November 2010. In reality, the trial didn't start until May 2, 2011.

I desperately wanted to move on, but it was difficult with this lingering on and on, month after month.

Finally, thankfully, the trail was set to begin, nearly 29 months after Taruk's body had been discovered.

Day 1 was an absolute trip. The first witness was Ian, who babbled and seemed frazzled throughout his testimony.

He sounded normal at the beginning when he described himself and his profession and education, but after that, nothing was straightforward. He stumbled and pondered with every answer.

I haven't been in a lot of courtrooms, but I've certainly never seen anyone behave with that decorum on the stand.

"What is your name?" he was asked.

"Um, OK, you mean the name that I was born with? Or what they called me in college?" Ian answered. "Oh my God, I've never been a witness before," he added.

Here's a man who is a lawyer. He knows exactly how the procedure works. He understands what's expected of a witness on the stand.

Or at least, he should.

But Ian acted confused the entire time. When asked if he had previously heard about Taruk's will,

Ian answered, "No, no, no." Then he stopped and acknowledged, "Yes, I'd heard of an instrument."

Ian's primary objective was to establish that he had a tight relationship with not only Hassan, but also Taruk. Ian insisted that he was doing all of this for them. He kept repeating, "The reason I'm here is because they asked me to be here; they asked me to be here at the end."

But Ian frequently misrepresented the truth, if not told outright lies, throughout his testimony. He insisted that the ownership of the building flip-flopped between Taruk and Hassan over the years. He wanted to try to make a case that Hassan's estate was worthy of inheriting the building for that reason.

His story was not true, though. Once Taruk bought his father out to save the building from being taken over by the bank, he was the exclusive owner, except for when he took a loan from his mom and temporarily gave her partial ownership in return.

Ian made great exaggerations about his relationship with Taruk, too. He said that he attended our wedding, but he was not there. Our wedding was in Las Vegas. He attended a reception back in Berkeley, but only because Hassan invited him.

Ian indicated that, in recent years before Taruk's disappearance, they had been hanging out at the gym together every day after work, at around 5 p.m. But Taruk always went to the gym in the morning before work. He came home after work to have dinner, relax and help Jordan with his homework.

Ian also said that even after Taruk had died, all of Taruk's long-time friends continued to contact him. When asked to name one, Ian singled out "Josh." One problem: Josh wasn't alive. He had committed suicide several years earlier.

The mistruths were endless. Ian claimed that he was involved in helping Taruk get a divorce from his first wife, Rebecca, when Taruk was much younger. But Taruk had told me that Rebecca got the marriage annulled, that he had nothing to do with it and didn't even know she was getting the annulment. They weren't married for long. It was yet another oddity, partly because Taruk was in jail during the time they were married.

Ian went on to say that he helped Taruk with a criminal case in 2003. During that time, he said that he met with Taruk once or twice a week to discuss legal issues involving a probation violation. But Taruk didn't have any legal problems in 2003. We were married by then.

During his testimony, Ian insisted that he wasn't involved in trying to negotiate any deals to keep the estate case from going to court. He claimed that he didn't call us to have a meeting at Sue's house back in late January/early February 2011 to discuss possible deals to split up the estate. Instead, Ian said, we had called him seeking advice because we knew nothing about handling a will and needed his expertise.

Ian, however, is a criminal attorney. He's not an estate attorney. I never would have even considered going to him for advice on this matter.

There were some other interesting items that came out of Ian's rambling testimony. He said that he had been told by Hassan that Taruk had moved to Minnesota. That's the first time most of us had heard that version of Hassan's lies. It was usually Mexico or Arizona.

Ian then gave his explanation for why Hassan had hidden Taruk's body, rather than inform the police. Hassan wrote in a letter that he had found Taruk dead from a drug overdose in a motel room.

According to Ian, Hassan covered it up because he was in trouble with the IRS for a debt going back some 40 years. Sue believed the same story.

Ian told the court that when one of his relatives died, he went to Taruk for counseling. Ian went on and on with these types of stories, many of them outright lies, trying to paint a picture that he and Taruk were such good friends. Maybe in Ian's mind, but not in reality. That's certainly not how Taruk felt about him.

Ian didn't even realize that Taruk had gone back to school to earn his Master of Social Work (MSW). Wouldn't such a close friend, as Ian kept describing himself, know something like that?

He also wasn't aware that Taruk had a daughter. His proposed deals didn't initially include Tiffany, because he didn't know about her. Wouldn't such a good buddy have known that, too?

Even Brad Johnson, Sue's husband, admitted that he thought Ian's testimony was odd.

Whether the judge considered Ian to be credible or not would be important to the case, because Ian testified that the signature on Taruk's purported will was indeed Taruk's handwriting and not a forgery.

I felt good that Ian had shown himself for what he is - completely unreliable with no credibility.

The next witness was Art, who described his relationship with his father, Hassan, and how they had ridden bicycles a couple of times a month for the last few years.

Art, who was about 4 years younger than Taruk, testified that Ian had tried to negotiate deals to keep us from going to court. Art said Sue informed him that Ian had completely left him out of one of the proposals.

Tina also testified over the phone that Ian had been negotiating deals. Tina confirmed that one of Ian's proposals to her was for Ian, Tiffany, Sue and me to split it up equally.

To me, both Art and Tina should have helped to discredit Ian even more. They both confirmed that Ian had flat-out lied about his role in trying to manufacture an out-of-court settlement.

His deals, of course, always included him taking a piece that he had no business receiving.

Day 2 in court began with a handwriting expert, Les Davie, called by Ian's attorney. Davie posted copies of signatures - multiple exemplars for both me and Taruk - on a big board.

Davie's approach centered on the "slants" and "leans" in the writing. I didn't see it. They all pretty much looked the same to me.

His finding, however, determined that it was "highly likely" that Taruk had signed the purported will. As for the "Wendy Ben-Ali" signature on the will, Davie indicated that it was likely I had signed it.

Davie used a scale that showed "highly unlikely" to the far left, "neutral" in the middle and "highly likely" to the far right.

The probability of Taruk's signature was listed on the far right while mine was toward the likely side, but two sections off of center, a sizable distance between the two of us. Davie definitely thought it was a better chance that Taruk's signature was real than mine.

I found it particularly interesting when my lawyer, Vernon Goins, managed to get Davie to confirm that he had received a letter from Ian's lawyer, Woody Goodman, telling him what they wanted the findings to be. Davie knew, going in, what he was supposed to find. It doesn't take Perry Mason to know that's just not right.

The cross examination by my lawyer was entertaining. It turned out that our handwriting expert, Jim White, had a run-in with their handwriting expert in the same court during another case. White wouldn't testify until the end of the trial, but Goins managed to pry out some intriguing background on White's rival, Davie.

Les Davie, it turned out, had been terminated by the Las Vegas Police Department for an alleged misconduct. Davie argued it wasn't for misconduct, but that he and one of his co-workers had a disagreement. He said the co-worker yelled at him, "I'll kill you."

Two managers overheard the dispute and because Davie's co-worker had more seniority, Davie was the one who was terminated.

I thought it was one of the stupidest explanations I'd ever heard. The other guy threatened him, but Davie was the one who was fired?

My lawyer, Goins, then asked Davie if he knew about Hassan's forgeries. Davie said that he had not seen any of the forged documents. Davie also said that he hadn't heard about the driver's license issued in Taruk's name and signed (actually forged by Hassan) in 2007, three years after Taruk disappeared.

After being shown the confirmed forgeries, Davie conceded there were some similarities between those and what was supposedly Taruk's signature on the purported will.

Goins told the court that he couldn't understand why Davie hadn't been made aware of some of this information. Good point.

Sue Johnson was next up on the stand. There were some intriguing pieces of information that came out in her testimony, not all involving the estate case.

She said that she was only married to Hassan from 1973 to '74, but that they lived off and on together for many years. Taruk was born in 1968. I didn't realize they were actually married for such a short period of time.

Sue confirmed that Taruk wasn't using drugs from 2000, when I first started dating him, through 2003, before relapsing in early '04.

When she was asked whether she took steps to locate Taruk during his four-year disappearance, she acknowledged that she did not.

It was an honest admission, but Sue wasn't truthful throughout. I just shook my head when she testified that Ian never suggested any out-of-court settlements and that he came to that meeting "to help us out."

My lawyer had an e-mail that Sue sent me that mentioned splitting things up 40 percent for her, 40 percent for me and 20 percent for Ian. The proposal was originated by Ian.

When Goins pressed her on these deals, she got frustrated, rolled her eyes and said that there was "a lot of fiddling with the numbers" going on during discussions.

Sue also came off looking bad when Goins asked her how much she paid in rent. She said that she paid $1,000 a month and that she always paid in cash.

"Are you sure you never paid by check?" Goins asked.

"I'm positive," Sue said.

"You never paid any money to Taruk monthly?" Goins said.

Sue again said no.

Goins then revealed a stack of checks that Sue had made out to Taruk on a monthly basis for $227, during the time when Taruk was missing. Hassan had taken the checks and either cashed or deposited them.

Much of Sue's testimony involved her previous ownership of the apartment complex. She had helped Taruk financially and, in the process, received 10 percent of the building on Sept. 13, 1995 and another eight percent on Oct. 1, 1996.

However, when she was very ill and hospitalized in 1999, Sue signed the 18 percent back over to Taruk. I had known that she wasn't too happy with Taruk for how that was handled.

That's why I felt from the start that she deserved something out of this estate - at the very least, that 18 percent back - even though we didn't always get along.

It was my turn to take the stand on the third day of the trial. I described the relationship between Taruk and myself, and also made it clear that Ian wasn't in our lives while I was with Taruk.

Ian's lawyer, Woody Goodman, asked me how much Taruk and I had discussed estate planning. I said we didn't talk about it. We never talked about dying. That wasn't something we dwelled on at our age.

What we did discuss was that owning the building assured Jordan and Tiffany would always have a place to live, if they needed it, and it could help us live comfortably in retirement.

Woodman tried to portray me as a money-hungry gold digger. He made a big deal about the fact that I had been out of work for three years and that I needed the money so desperately. I was strangely singled out from everyone in that way, even though I don't think I needed the money any more than the others.

"You just want the money," Woodman said to me on the stand.

I was amazed that I had to defend myself in this way. This was my husband's estate, after all. I don't think it's a reach to think I deserved a part of it, just like Tiffany and Sue did.

I definitely deserved it much more than Ian and Art, that's for sure.

But lawyers are going to do whatever they have to in order to win a case for their client.

"That's more than a million dollars," Goodman said to me. "Isn't that a lot of money?"

I told him everything is relative and that I wasn't there just for the money.

First of all, it wasn't really a million dollars. At the most, I would split the estimated $1.5 million estate with Tiffany. I wasn't planning to sell the building, either, so there was going to be a hefty mortgage to pay.

When it came down to crunching numbers, in terms of short-term income, you're talking about maybe $1,200 or so per month in revenue from the rent. That isn't a lot of money.

Having the building as an asset would give me and Jordan some potential long-term security. I think Taruk would have wanted that. In fact, I know Taruk would have wanted that.

It was disgusting to me that they would challenge my motives. I was a widow. I had been through a lot. First with my husband's drug relapse, then with his disappearance for 4 1/2 years, and then the revelation that he was dead, killed by his father and buried in a wall.

Jordan, my son, lost the father figure in his life. He had been through so much, too. Did we really have to justify inheriting some of Taruk's assets?

To me, it seemed to indicate that Ian and his lawyer were desperate.

The only concern I really had after my testimony was that when I was asked about the "Wendy Ben-Ali" signature on Taruk's purported will, I admitted, "The Wendy looks good. It does. That really looks like my writing. I just never wrote 'Ben-Ali.'"

The other side, naturally, would argue that my statement suggests I had signed it, but I didn't. Had I seen that will, I never would have signed it. I would have said, "Taruk, where is the insurance policy with me as the beneficiary? How come it's not written in the will?"

To leave all of that to his father instead of his new bride would have been insulting to me.

I simply never saw the will. I never signed the will. I believe somebody had forged my name, and to be honest, they did a pretty darn good job of it.

After I finished testifying, my lawyer felt that there wasn't enough evidence to prove the will was valid, so he attempted to get the case thrown out.

The judge, Mason Whitman, a black man in his mid-50s, made it clear that it wouldn't be in our best interests to seek a ruling at that point.

"I have a will here," Judge Whitman said. "Everything at face value, it looks like a proper will to me. It would not behoove you to make a decision right now. Right now, everything looks fine to me."

Unfortunately, this statement made my under-lining feelings more relevant. I had feared, as the trial moved on, that this judge had a preconceived notion or bias against my side. I hoped that I was being paranoid, but his reaction certainly wasn't a good sign for us.

Vernon said the judge's decision was typical, that they normally won't throw out a case so easily at that point, but he felt it was worth taking a shot. Vernon was always calm and reassuring, which I needed because the process was getting frustrating for me.

We moved on to Day 4. The final witness who was scheduled to take the stand was Jim White, the handwriting expert for my side. As far as I know, he had not been informed of what we wanted his findings to be.

Clearly, I'm biased, but I really thought White's presentation was much better than Davie's.

For instance, White made exact measurements to determine the length of, say, a swoop in a given signature. You could visually see the point he was making, which I didn't think was the case with Davie.

On the scale that ranged from highly unlikely on one side to highly likely on the other, White ruled that the signatures for both Taruk and I being real were on the unlikely end.

White also concluded that, based on Hassan's other known forgeries, it was likely that Hassan had also forged Taruk's signature on the purported will. "More than 50 percent likelihood," White stated.

There were only two examples of a Wendy "Ben-Ali" signature to compare. The one I signed for the timeshare while Taruk and I were in Las Vegas getting married, and the one on his purported will.

Based on the dates on the two documents, these signatures would have been signed about two weeks apart.

Nevertheless, the "Ben-Ali" part looked absolutely nothing alike.

White went on to explain the three different ways that are typically used to forge a signature. One is with tracing, another is cut-and-paste and the other way is a simulation.

White's theory was that the signature for Taruk on the purported will was a "rapid simulation," where the forger is looking at someone's writing and trying to write it as closely as possible. He felt that is what Hassan attempted with Taruk's will.

White said that he also found Hassan's forgery on one of the loans to be similar to the signature on the purported will. He called that "highly likely."

The controversy involving the handwriting experts continued. White had apparently been kicked out of some forensic handwriting organization. Watching the lawyers attack the handwriting experts was somewhat humorous.

At the end of all the witness testimonies, Judge Whitman followed up with some questions of his own. He requested that White take the stand again.

Judge Whitman said he wanted to go over the similarities between Hassan's known forgeries to the Taruk signature on the purported will. He went on with White for probably 15 more minutes.

I started to think that maybe the judge was really listening to my side and thought White was providing scientific evidence. I became hopeful that I had been wrong earlier about Judge Whitman and that he was starting to lean in our favor.

The trial was originally supposed to last three days and it went into a fourth. There was even talk of a fifth day, but the consensus opposed that move.

The judge gave the lawyers the option of returning for another day or to give their closing arguments in writing. The lawyers agreed to write them. They were told to present their five-page arguments within a week.

About a month later, we received the judge's ruling. The lawyers for Ian, Sue and Art had to prove the will was valid, and the judge, believe it or not, determined they did.

Here were some of the key points that came out with his decision:

1. Judge Whitman obviously didn't care that the second witness on the will couldn't be found because the signature was illegible.

2. He also overlooked the fact that the address read "2235 Ashby #201 Berkeley, CA." That was the address for the apartment building, but I never lived there. I never would have used that address.

3. He said my forged signature on the purported will looked exactly like my true signature on the timeshare agreement. I thought the "Ben-Ali" parts were as different as night and day.

4. The judge believed it was Taruk's signature on the purported will because Ian had said so. Judge Whitman actually considered Ian credible. Unbelievable.

5. Judge Whitman also felt it actually made sense that Taruk would have written a will on the day before going on his honeymoon, and still left nearly his entire estate to his dad. The judge believed the will truly was Taruk's intention.

As a side note, Judge Whitman did rule that Ian, despite being the alternate executor on the will, could not fulfill that role because of his conduct in trying to negotiate out-of-court deals.

It left Duane Leonard, who had been previously appointed by the court to replace me, to continue in his role as special administrator for the estate.

Based on Judge Whitman's ruling, Tiffany and I would receive nothing from the estate.

By declaring Taruk's will valid, it meant that Hassan's estate would inherit Taruk's estate, and Sue would get everything.

It didn't seem right. In retrospect, the logical solution would have been for me, Tiffany and Sue to split up the estate in some manner. Perhaps 20 percent for Sue, 40 percent for both me and Tiffany.

We had discussed a settlement that included the three of us before the trial, but Sue didn't want to deal with Tina (Tiffany's mom), because Tina was talking about trying to sell the building. Sue, of course, lives in the building. Tina and Tiffany live on the other side of the country.

Tina, meanwhile, didn't want Art to be left out of any agreement and I strongly opposed Art being included.

In the end, we weren't able to get on the same page. It looked like a mistake made by Tina and I, based on this judge's ruling, but I never, not in my wildest imagination, believed that the will would be ruled valid by a court.

Inevitably, there's going to be an appeal, which would be handled much differently, with no lawyers, no witnesses, no trial involved.

It's all handled on paper and based on the cases already presented. Three appellant judges would be assigned, which I like. I can't believe there would be three other judges who would find that will valid and believe that those were Taruk's true wishes.

Nevertheless, I was dumbfounded by Judge Whitman's decision. I feared the worst based on my gut feeling about him, but it was still stunning to hear.

While I assumed that it was obvious that Ian wasn't credible, my lawyer informed me that the judge thought I was the one who wasn't credible.

It's difficult to know exactly what went wrong. Did the history between the two handwriting experts in the same courtroom a few months earlier have any effect? I wonder, but I guess I'll never know the truth.

Despite the disappointment, I invited Sue over the following week for Jordan's high-school graduation party. She gave him a very generous gift, which was much appreciated.

"No congratulations," Sue said in reference to the trial. "I don't know what's going to happen. You know how this has been going. There's no reason to celebrate."

If she indeed inherits the entire estate, it will be interesting to see whether she gives a portion to Tiffany, perhaps even to Jordan.

Either way, we'll be all right. The money, obviously, would be nice. We can use it. But it honestly never was just about the money.

The fact is, I did not sign the will. It wasn't what Taruk would have wanted. I know that for a fact.

For Sue to fight me through all this, I think was horrible. It made the terrible nightmare that much longer and that much worse.

# CHAPTER 9

Having lived a lie, it was only appropriate for Hassan Ben-Ali to leave behind one more lie in the letter he wrote before his suicide. It once again summed up his pathetic life.

A few people who were close to him bought his story that he had found his son dead of a drug overdose in an Oakland motel room, but I am convinced that it was just another of Hassan's fabrications.

I strongly believe that Taruk was murdered. Either by Hassan himself, someone Hassan paid (Waldo, who had cashed thousands of dollars in apparent extortion checks from Hassan) or, quite possibly, both of them.

Based on Taruk's track record, I understand how a drug overdose sounds feasible. But I am adamant that it was not an overdose, not after talking to him that same morning. If we hadn't talked over the phone, I would feel much different.

That was the first time Taruk had ever shown such sincere remorse and explained to me in detail how he felt about what he was doing to himself and to us. There was no guarantee that he would live up to his promise long-term, but I think his clear mind and positive attitude would have carried him for a while, certainly for the rest of that day at the very least.

It sounded to me like he had put a great deal of thought into his decision to seek help for his drug problem. He had also come to terms with the fact that he had to find a way to remove Hassan's negativity from his life and from our lives.

So that's my rationale for why it was murder as opposed to overdose. My lawyer is still planning a wrongful death claim, which we hadn't done previously because Hassan's estate was worth only $328 before inheriting Taruk's $1.5 million estate, based on the judge's ruling. If it's declared to be a wrongful death, then the estate would at least go to the right people, including me.

I simply refuse to believe that Taruk went straight from our conversation to OD'ing in a motel room by himself hours later. He had established a pattern and that was not the norm.

I think I was probably the last person to talk with Taruk, other than Hassan and maybe Waldo. Based on that talk, I think it's more likely that Taruk immediately went to confront his father on several issues.

Maybe he told Hassan to stay out of our lives, or that he didn't want his dad managing the building anymore, or even demanded that he move out of the apartment complex, who knows?

But when Taruk tried to draw the line, I think that Hassan realized the only way to stay in control was to get rid of Taruk. I believe that building caused all of this to happen. If there was no building, then Taruk wouldn't be dead. There would be no reason to hide him.

His dad's obsession with money and the building led to this tragedy. It was a dysfunctional family gone bad in the worst way possible, with money becoming more important than human lives, including that of his own son.

A month before Taruk disappeared, his father had taken him on that trip to Mexico. Hassan's plan all along was to talk Taruk into dumping his family. Hassan tried to convince him to get a divorce during that trip, but it didn't work.

Hassan had been so noticeably happy - attempting to appear nurturing, while at the same time, offering to pay me off - when he told me that Taruk wanted a divorce a few weeks after he went missing. It's clear to me that Hassan was the spawn of the devil.

Why was he so giddy over the idea of a divorce? It's what he wanted for Taruk, going back to our wedding day and even earlier. It's so sad. Taruk was truly in love for the first time, happy to have a family of his own. And his father wanted to sabotage and poison everything that Taruk and I were building.

Hassan made sure that Sue relayed a story, another of his lies, to me in 2006 that Taruk had met a nice white woman and had fallen in love with her. Sue said that Hassan liked her a lot and thought she and Taruk were such a happy couple. Sue said that Hassan was "elated" for Taruk.

Hassan then went on to convince everyone - from Hasira to Art to Ian - that Taruk and I were divorced. It was part of his grand scheme to set up the fake will and make sure others bought into it.

I received tremendous resistance. They all believed that Taruk and I were divorced and questioned why I was even involved in the estate at all. I actually had to prove to them that I was still married to Taruk.

It's amazing how anybody can believe anything Hassan ever said, but a lot of people who were close to him really did believe the motel overdose story about Taruk.

I refuse to believe it and it makes me angry that any of them do. I was in the hotel business for 30 years, and a dead body being removed isn't likely to go unnoticed.

My theory on what happened comes down to three possibilities, based on educated opinions:

1. A sleeper move was used to make Taruk unconscious. Taruk was bigger and stronger than both Hassan and Waldo. There was no way they could physically overpower him.

A sleeper hold, however, can render a person unconscious in as little as five seconds. It is performed by wrapping an arm around the person's neck to restrict air and blood flow.

I had never even heard of a sleeper until I met these people. But I had seen them do it and I know Hassan was capable of pulling it off. It was the best way, perhaps the only way, that he could have handled Taruk quickly with no violent confrontation.

To put him in a sleeper hold, he didn't have to overpower him at all. He just had to have him in the right position.

If Taruk's back was turned, Hassan could have grabbed him and put him in a sleeper hold so fast, Taruk wouldn't have been able to respond.

After Taruk was unconscious, they could have suffocated him by covering his mouth and nose.

2. Another possibility is Taruk was given the date-rape drug in a drink to knock him out.

3. Finally, it's conceivable that a towel soaked in chloroform was used to cover Taruk's mouth and nose, another way to put him to sleep without making a sound.

I have no evidence of any of this, but there's also no evidence that Taruk committed suicide with an overdose, other than Hassan's word, which means nothing.

Hassan's story took place at a motel in Oakland. I have a hard time believing that they could move Taruk, who weighed about 250 pounds, out of that motel, into a car and over to the apartment building without someone noticing. Hassan weighed about 160 pounds, and Waldo 175 pounds.

There's one other person, Terry, who could have helped those two. Terry was older, but he was bigger and stronger. He was a former drug addict who did a lot of manual labor for Hassan, the equivalent of an indentured servant.

Sue told me that Terry helped to build the casket, but she protected him during the initial police investigation. I've always wondered how much more Terry knew.

Here's another unanswered question: How did Hassan know to go to this motel room in the first place to supposedly find Taruk's body? Obviously, someone from the motel didn't call him or they would have notified police. Did Taruk, drugged out of his mind, call him right before he died? Possible. But the last time he was in dire straits, Taruk called me, not Hassan.

I just don't see how Hassan's version could have occurred in only a matter of hours after I talked to Taruk. He was too lucid and upbeat to take such a drastic turn so quickly. That's not how it had worked with him when he'd have a relapse.

Unfortunately, there was no way for police to try to determine which motel to check for a surveillance video. Taruk was dead, Hassan was dead and Waldo couldn't be located.

I do not rule out the possibility that Taruk was buried alive. I believe the crime took place at 2235 Ashby Ave. I think Taruk was held captive in that bunker at the apartment building, either dead or alive. Hassan had locked him up in the bunker before.

Another enigma to me is how Hassan could have torn out a wall in the apartment building without anyone hearing or noticing anything going on?

We called that downstairs area "the bunker," which was a pet name for what was really a small converted storage area. It had a loft and a desk, no windows, no entryway. You dead-bolted the room from the outside.

The bunker was adjacent to where Taruk's body was found. After hiding Taruk in the wall, Hassan changed the bunker around, removing the loft and desk and turning it back into a storage room, its original purpose, where he kept his bicycle.

I assume even Hassan started feeling some guilt and couldn't regularly bear looking at the room. That's why Hassan switched the bunker back to a storage room.

Sue Johnson argues that Hassan never would have harmed Taruk in any way, much less murdered him and even buried him alive, because he loved his son.

For me, Sue's claims fall on deaf ears when she talks about Hassan's devotion to Taruk. I couldn't even talk to her at times when she tried to glorify Hassan and make Taruk the bad guy. Taruk was not the bad guy. He had his problems, but he was the victim in the end.

Sue had the audacity to characterize what Hassan did by hiding his son's body as merely "an error in judgment."

Error in judgment? What in blue hell is she talking about?

At the very least, hiding the body in that manner was a crime, not to mention all the fraud that ensued.

I wish that Sue would have stopped trying to protect Hassan and been honest with herself and everyone else.


Since June 8, 2004, the day Taruk went missing and presumably was killed, I've replayed in my mind every little detail going back to the day we met.

Obviously, I have regrets. At the top of the list was that I didn't take Taruk seriously enough when he talked about moving to Las Vegas.

I told him, "You have a job, I have a job, we're settled, we love the Bay Area, and I don't want to uproot Jordan. Besides, it's too hot in Vegas."

To uproot everyone because he couldn't tell his dad to leave us alone? At the time, I thought that was ridiculous, but it doesn't seem so ridiculous now.

If we had moved, this never would have happened. Something else might have happened if Taruk couldn't overcome his drug problem, but not anything like this.

If I had just moved, it could have been different. I've gone through the woulda-coulda-shoulda syndrome over and over.

I did ask my boss about possibly moving at the time, because Taruk brought up the idea more than just in passing. My boss gave me the go-ahead to move anywhere in my territory, which included Nevada. So I could have done it.

I just didn't want to. That was the bottom line. Never, not in a million years, did I think it could come to this.

In retrospect, wanting to move was Taruk's way of trying to break away from his dad. That's absolutely what it was. That was the whole thing. I didn't see it back then, but I can see it clearly now.

There had been so many times over the years when Taruk had said, "I just don't want my dad in our life." But then he'd let Hassan right back in to create problems for him and for us.

It took time for him to get to the point where he could draw a line in the sand with his dad. I think Taruk was finally coming to terms with the whole game, the racket his dad had going on.

I guess he thought the easiest way to get away from it all was to move out of town, to get as far away from Hassan as possible. I just thought that was a copout, that he should be stronger and deal with it. I thought he should be able to just say, "Leave me alone," and stick by it.

It didn't work like that for him. His father had the power to maneuver his way back in just when it seemed Taruk was pushing him away.

If he had talked about moving somewhere other than Vegas - Portland or Seattle would have been ideal spots for us to start over - maybe my reaction would have been different.

Considering the drug element, I'm not sure the fast pace of Vegas would have been the answer.

Being around that lifestyle all the time might have been too detrimental to him.

I just wish that I would have considered it more at the time and offered some other options, like Portland or Seattle, anything to get Taruk away from Hassan. That's what needed to happen.

In some ways, I feel like I lost 4 1/2 years of my life during this ordeal. At the same time, I learned so much about myself and other people.

My mother helped to teach me about the different stages of the mourning process - from anger, to denial, to bargaining, to depression, to acceptance. I went through all of those twice. She helped to guide me through it the first time, when Taruk disappeared, because I had no idea how to handle it.

I was a basket case, driving her crazy. We were constantly on the phone, hours and hours of crying and asking, "What could have happened? Why would he do this?"

She finally told me, "You're going to have to treat this as if he's gone, dead. That's the only way you're going to get over it. If you don't, then you're just going to wallow in this forever. You have no idea where he is. His dad says he's gone, so let's just make him gone."

Once I learned the different stages of grieving, I acknowledged them and worked my way through each part. I had trouble with denial, or at least it seemed like denial at the time because, in the back of my mind, I always expected Taruk to surface again one day.

It's difficult to go through the steps of mourning when you don't think the person is really dead. You have to try to trick your mind. I basically went through the steps of mourning a loss. Instead of thinking that he was dead, I went through the steps as if I had lost something. I've lost this person; I'm never going to see him again.

When I found out that he was really dead, I went through the steps again but differently. Even though what had happened to him and how it happened was a shock, his loss was no longer a shock. I hadn't seen him in 4 1/2 years.

The first mourning was much harder. There was no warning, no reason, no explanation. I prayed that he would return soon and be OK, but it almost killed me to go through it. I was that messed up mentally.

The second time, even though he was really dead, at least I knew the truth. If someone is dead, they're dead. You deal with it. You go through mourning. Some people never get over the death of a loved one, but at least they know that they're dead. There's no uncertainty, no wondering if they're going to return at any moment.

Intense anger for Hassan was a big part of the second mourning. My self-esteem was severely damaged when I thought Taruk had abandoned us, but I had gone through all of that only because of Hassan's lie. None of it was real.

While it seemed like I was in such denial about him leaving me, in the end, I really wasn't. What I wanted to believe after he had disappeared was right. He did not leave me.

One of Taruk's favorite phrases was "Life on life's terms." He would tell that to Jordan a lot. You have to deal with whatever life throws at you. Taruk said that it built character and strength.

The reality is that you don't have a choice. Unless, of course, you check out like Hassan did by pulling a trigger to his head or if you end up on drugs like Taruk did.

Other people may have other vices, like alcohol or shopping, or perhaps an eating disorder such as bulimia. There are many types of these problems that people create in their lives, because sometimes, reality is just too painful for them.

But you have to reach down and find a way to overcome whatever it is, and that's what I had to do. I heard Taruk's voice in my head, repeating that line, "Life on life's terms. Be strong, deal with it."

It took me until 2008, during the second mourning process, before I accepted that I needed to seek professional therapy to help me through. I had thought it was a sign of weakness if you needed to talk to someone about your problems.

Even though that's what Taruk did for a living, I didn't totally believe in the industry, at least not for myself.

But my therapist helped me to understand that it's OK to be weak and broken. It's only when you accept that about yourself that you can rebuild. I still think it depends on who you speak to, but I was fortunate; my doctor was very good and helped me a lot.

What did I learn about myself? One of the most important realizations, which explains why I found myself in some bad relationships, is that, while I wanted to believe in people and wanted to believe that they're capable of change, the truth is that I was a caretaker and an enabler.

If I could do it all over again, I wouldn't ignore the red flags like I did many times. I would question, if not seriously doubt, that someone with a history of bad decision-making has truly changed.

I definitely wouldn't get involved with someone who was a habitual hardcore drug user, because that side can emerge again at the first hint of adversity, especially if they are so close to their triggers as Taruk was to his dad. I also wouldn't drink with a person who has a severe drug history. While it might be social drinking for you and me, it can be the calm before the storm for them.

I made some poor choices in relationships. They weren't all necessarily classic bad boys, but I do think I'm a risk-taker. I felt that I could fix people. I realize now that I can't, especially if they don't want to be fixed.

When you're in a relationship, problems don't always immediately surface. It takes time to really get to know someone to their core. You also have to accept some shortcomings. No one is perfect.

Once I saw the red flags, I typically did start planning my exit. But in Taruk's case, I was fooled into believing that his drug life was all behind him. I really didn't see it ever emerging again. I thought he had grown out of it.

You can say that I trust too easily and blindly, but you want to think the best in others. You don't want to be the type that is constantly judging everyone you meet. Only God can judge me. I believe in that for myself, so I believe in it for others as well.

Still, in some cases, it would have been better for me to walk away sooner. Every time I thought that I could change someone, I was wrong.

I know now that I didn't look closely and seriously enough at the backgrounds of these men. I probably also ignored my instincts too much at times, those inner whispers that can help to guide you through life if you listen close enough.

As Oprah would say, "When you feel the pebble, don't wait until the entire brick wall falls on you."

I have only myself to blame for getting into some of these bad relationships. If someone has an unhealthy situation with their family, which was a factor in all of my bad relationships, then I need to identify that as a big red flag. You have to look at it as an indication of who they will be. After all, we're each a product of our environments.

Some people, understandably, are going to think it's strange that I would still want to own the apartment building after everything that has happened. But I see it as a way to keep Taruk's dream alive.

As crazy as things got over there at times, there was a part of Taruk that really enjoyed owning it.

He didn't want to sell it. In fact, he wanted to live there.

I wouldn't have anything to do with that, not with his mom and dad still there. When Taruk asked me to move in there, as many of his girlfriends had done before me, I wondered if he thought I was crazy.

Believe it or not, we had thrown around the possibility of moving in after we retired. By the time we were in our 60s, who knew where Hassan and Sue would be in their lives and whether their personalities would have changed by then. To be honest, I thought they probably wouldn't be mobile enough at that age to bother us too much, even if that's what they wanted to do.

So I hadn't ruled out moving there someday, as long as the crazy characters were gone and the wild nightlife had subsided.

To Taruk, the building represented security for Jordan and Tiffany. Taruk had a big heart. As long as he could assure them that they would always have a place to live, no matter where they were in their lives, then that made him feel good.

After everything that's happened, I do still want to own the building. I know it sounds crazy, but out of respect for Taruk and knowing that he died because of the building, I would not want to sell it.

For me to inherit the building, or part of it, and sell it just for the money would be wrong in my mind. Why not keep it and do exactly what Taruk wanted for it?

While I could never live there and have no desire to even go back there, Jordan actually has talked about being the manager. Taruk had told Jordan that he would always have an apartment there for him, no matter what.

It might be a moot point based on the judge's initial ruling on the estate, but I think that Jordan would feel like he would be living up to Taruk's wishes, and doing what his dad did for a while, if he lived there and managed it. I think that actually would make Jordan feel proud. Jordan also wants to follow in Taruk's footsteps by pursuing psychology and social work. Despite everything that happened, Taruk definitely left a positive impact on Jordan.

I'm so thankful that Jordan never saw or experienced Taruk's dark side, that I was able to protect him from it. Only in recent years has Jordan heard about some of Taruk's demons.

So, in Jordan's eyes, Taruk will always be a nearly perfect father to him.

It would be way too creepy for me to live in the Ashby building - I don't see how Sue does it - but the idea doesn't seem to bother Jordan. Of course, he could feel different and change his mind if it ever really happened.

Maybe if I could ask Taruk now, "How do you feel after being hidden in there for 4 1/2 years?" he might say, "Sell that thing as quick as you can."

I don't know, but I do know that when he was living, he looked at it like a nest egg for all of us. I don't know if it's going to happen now, but I would actually like to keep that going in Taruk's memory.

From my perspective, selling the building just to have half a million dollars to go travel around and buy things, would be an extension of Hassan's greed.

If Sue Johnson indeed ends up inheriting the building, I doubt that she'll sell it, either. She'll continue to live there.

Hopefully, she'll honor Taruk's wishes and have a standing offer to Jordan and Tiffany to live there, if either ever wants or needs to.

As Taruk's widow, it's hard for me to accept that I won't be awarded any of his assets based on everything I know.

My lawyer is still going to ask for family support from the estate to help pay for Jordan's college tuition. It would be money to cover Taruk's financial contribution to us while he was missing.

We are asking for $90,000, which would be outside of the will being declared valid or invalid. The special administrator would make the sole decision.

I'm not holding my breath, but I pray that somehow the truth gets proven about how Taruk died. I believe that I know, but I want everyone to know.

The only chance, it seems, for that to happen is if the police locate Waldo and he comes clean. They say that they're looking for him. There have been some hints as to his whereabouts, but no definite sightings. Maybe somehow, someway, someday Waldo will step forward with the whole story.

Writing this book has done a great deal of good for my spirit. It helped put everything in perspective and healed me some, too, in the process.

I felt the story had to be told. If one person learns something and doesn't make the same mistakes, then it will be worth it.

My advice: If you have issues in your life, don't keep them a secret because you're embarrassed to ask for help like I did. It's too hard to deal with major issues alone. Family, friends, and professional therapists are there and want to help.

I guess that once the appeal and the court case are completely over, and Taruk's wishes have been fulfilled, I will be at peace. I can close this chapter on my life, and finally move on.

Taruk was a great loss to me and to Jordan. I believe we had a chance to be happy again despite Taruk's struggles. I had hoped that we could get him the help he needed with a drug-rehabilitation program that he would have participated in for the rest of his life, so he could deal with those "demons" on a daily basis.

Unfortunately for us, there was another demon at work. Hassan took Taruk's life and he changed mine and Jordan's dramatically. Sometimes "life on life's terms" isn't fair.

# CHAPTER 10

After the horror of being buried for so long inside that wall, Taruk needed a proper resting place. I organized a memorial service for January 10, 2009, a little over three weeks after his body was found.

About 30 of us, including 10 of Taruk's childhood friends, gathered on a windy day at the Berkeley Pier to say farewell and to spread Taruk's ashes into the Pacific Ocean. Taruk had said that he wanted to be cremated.

He hated funerals more than anything. He didn't even go to his grandmother's service. We wanted to keep it simple, which was what Taruk would have preferred, but we had to do something to recognize his life and what he'd gone through.

It was not your typical memorial service with a minister, but it was an emotional tribute. We took turns, with nearly everyone saying something to honor Taruk.

It was the first time I even met most of those friends from his wild days as a delinquent youth. They had all moved on with their lives. Sue helped me to get in touch with them. I was grateful they came to pay their respects.

Pastor David, a teenage friend of Taruk's, talked about how they used to get into fights and were constantly in trouble. He said it had been satisfying to watch all the changes in everyone and to see them all settle down over the years.

A friend of mine, Ivonne Calderon, told a story about Taruk counseling her through some adversity. He made her realize that she was important, that the rough times would go away, and that she just had to be strong. Ivonne was in tears as she described how Taruk had made a difference in her life.

The most emotional part of the ceremony came when Jordan spoke openly to Taruk. Jordan said he missed him dearly, but hoped he was finally at peace. It broke my heart to see Jordan's pain.

I had written a poem for Taruk, but I couldn't even talk after hearing Jordan's speech. I had to have Ivonne read it out loud for me.

Sue chose not to speak and didn't even cry. I had a hard time understanding the lack of emotion on her part.

JJ brought champagne for everyone. We gave a toast to Taruk before scattering his ashes in the water, along with some tiny diamonds and miniature Chevy Chevelle and Nissan cars. Taruk liked to wear jewelry and absolutely loved cars.

Before going to lunch, we handed roses to everyone to drop into the water. There was a strong breeze coming off the Bay that morning, carrying the roses one-by-one toward the Golden Gate Bridge and into the Pacific Ocean.

You would think that one rose might veer to the right, another to the left. But those roses actually formed a single file as they floated away from the pier. It was a picturesque scene and a touching moment.

I don't know if it was merely coincidence, or if maybe there was some subtle message from above, but the trail of those roses warmed my heart.

I felt as if Taruk, after living so much of his life surrounded by turmoil and insanity, had finally found some semblance of tranquility.

Made in the USA
Lexington, KY
12 June 2012